A Poetry of Two Minds

The Life of Poetry:

POETS ON THEIR ART AND CRAFT

A Poetry of Two Minds

Sherod Santos

The University of Georgia Press
ATHENS AND LONDON

Published by the University of Georgia Press
Athens, Georgia 30602
© 2000 by Sherod Santos
All rights reserved
Designed by Erin Kirk New
Set in 11.5 on 14 Centaur by G&S Typesetters
Printed and bound by Maple-Vail

The paper in this book meets the guidelines for
permanence and durability of the Committee on
Production Guidelines for Book Longevity of the
Council on Library Resources.

Printed in the United States of America

04 03 02 01 00 C 5 4 3 2 1

04 03 02 01 00 P 5 4 3 2 1

Library of Congress Cataloging-in-Publication Data

Santos, Sherod, 1948–
A poetry of two minds / Sherod Santos.
   p. cm.—(The life of poetry)
Includes bibliographical references.
ISBN 0-8203-224-X (alk. paper)
ISBN 0-8203-2204-0 (pbk. : alk. paper)
1. American poetry—20th century—History and criticism.
2. Poetry. I. Title. II. Series.
PS323.5.S26 2000
811'.509—dc21

                                99-057977

British Library Cataloging-in-Publication Data available

for Lynne

Contents

Preface

It goes without saying that when poets are writing about rather than writing poetry they're engaged in an activity very different in kind from the one they're most accustomed to: not necessarily subordinate to it, but nonetheless somehow significantly other. The degree and nature of that difference, however, may not be quite so apparent. The famous terms W. H. Auden employed—the sacred and the profane ("the value of a profane thing lies in what it usefully does, the value of a sacred thing lies in what it *is*")—are less likely to serve as satisfactory distinctions to the more high-minded theorists of the day. Or to those who feel that criticism has risen to the status of an art while art has descended to the moribund status of an ideological tool.

But perhaps we'll find some basis for agreement around the neutral position that in both poetry and criticism something lays claim to our attention, however different those claims may be. Less fitful than tenacious, less exploratory than cartographic, less willy-nilly than intentional, the poetry essay takes as its subject the very thing that poetry withholds, even from those who write it: the confounding problem of what it is, or how it came to be what it is, or how "what it is" has been determined by psychological forces within the poet, aesthetic forces within the literary tradition, or value-laden forces within the culture at large. Whatever the case, these are versions of itself which poetry, in the act of being made, instinctively struggles to unmake, for in order to *become* something in the moment, the poem must resist *being* what it was a moment before. It must escape that image reflected in the mirror the essay would hold up to it.

"The secret of poetry is never explained," Emerson wrote at

seventy-two, in a last entry in his journals, and I suspect that anyone who has pondered those secrets has come to a similar conclusion. But as anyone who has kept a secret has also come to know, the more powerful the secret, the more urgently it longs to be told. What that means for the poet writing about poetry is, of course, a complicated matter, for whatever fresh knowledge one claims as a critic, one must, in turn, disclaim as a poet. The poet must become, as Stevens reminds us, "an ignorant man again."

Be that as it may, in the most fortuitous and self-revealing moments, the common element these genres share can suddenly outreach that paradox. If we view the imagination as a submarine world filled with myriad unheard-of creatures—creatures which, from some unsounded depth within us, swim up to the surface of our attention—then perhaps we can view these brief incursions as a kind of underwater sonar, pulsations sent out into the oceanic dark in the hope of finding an echo. Indeed, at various times while writing this book I've felt like one of a small but devoted community intent on exploring that submarine realm.

The bulk of these pieces have resulted from invitations to address, in person or on the page, certain groups within that community, and in keeping with that purpose I've tried to adapt them to the length, tone, and topic of the occasion. The initial essay, for example, was first delivered as a talk to a community writers' group in Shreveport, Louisiana; the tribute to Robinson Jeffers derives from an address to the Jeffers Festival in Carmel, California; the essays on translation and Orpheus grew out of seminars I taught at the University of Missouri; the ones on Baudelaire and angels had their beginnings in a series of talks I gave in Northern Ireland. "Divine Hunger," on the other hand, is the result of eight or nine years of random, infrequent note-taking on a subject suggested by a seminar I audited at the University of California-Irvine, a seminar composed of nine brilliantly mischievous lectures by that unlikely muse Jacques Derrida. Still others arose from questions that either puzzled or beleaguered me long enough that I finally sat down to think them through.

While I've tried to arrange the collection to reflect the development of certain ideas I've wrestled with over the years, the methodical reader may feel frustrated to find that, taken on the whole, it shows little evidence of a single, sustained critical perspective; and, as if to further frustrate that reader, it exhibits more interest in questions than in answers. While stubbornly maintaining a handful of contending hypotheses, I've resisted the instinct to normalize, from one piece to another, the arguments on which they're based.

Having said that, I should also say that whatever revisions I've made since the essays first appeared in print were prompted by a kind of mind-clearing logic which could only have come belatedly, and only by virtue of a new internal reckoning suggested by the tropes, ideas, subjects, and opinions that recur throughout the whole.

Chief among those recurrences is the odd but enduring impression that poems have minds of their own, minds frequently indifferent to, independent of, and on occasion blithely inaccessible to the mind that's marshaled to compose them. I'm speaking, of course, about lyric poetry (though the collection will touch on other types as well), that form which finds its dramatic character in the field of linguistic action and its *mimesis* in the structure of the mind in thought. Accordingly, these essays represent repeated, sometimes haphazard attempts to explore not only what I think about poetry but what it is, and how it is, poetry thinks about itself. What follows, then, is a matter of two minds, minds related by their differences, if still different in their kind.

Acknowledgments

I'm indebted to a number of people for their insights, nudgings, and sure-handed editorial suggestions. Most particularly I want to thank Lynne McMahon, whose thinking helped form, as well as inform, these essays, and Herb Leibowitz, who has set, by example, a very high standard for the literary essay. I also want to thank the stars for providing me with such an intrepid and intelligent poet-editor, Barbara Ras, who, having encouraged me to put this collection together in the first place, had the fortitude to follow it through to the end. This book would not exist without her.

A number of these essays have been published elsewhere. Many have been revised or retitled since their first appearances; a few have been significantly expanded. For their interest and energies, I'm grateful to the editors of the following publications:

"A Toy Balloon, the Man-Moth's Tear, and a Sack of Ripe Tomatoes": as "Poetry and Attention," *New England Review* 9, no. 3 (spring 1987).

"On the Memory of Stone": published in chapbook form by The Robinson Jeffers Tor House Foundation (Bath NY: Foothills Publishing, 1997).

"A Story of Poetry and Poets": *Kenyon Review* 18, no. 1 (winter 1996).

"Writing the Poet, Unwriting the Poem": as "An Art of Poetry," in *What Will Suffice: Contemporary American Poets on the Art of Poetry*, ed. Christopher Buckley and Christopher Merrill (Salt Lake City: Gibbs-Smith Publishers, 1995).

"Shelley in Ruins": in *Touchstones,* ed. Robert Pack and Jay Parini (Middlebury: Middlebury College Press, 1995).

"Eating the Angel, Conceiving the Sun": *American Poetry Review* 22, no. 6 (November/December 1993); reprinted in *The Pushcart Prize, XVIII: Best of the Small Presses, 1993–94* (Wainscott NY: Pushcart Press, 1994).

"Divine Hunger": *Kenyon Review* 22, no. 1/winter 2000.

"'Into the Unknown to Find the New'": *American Poetry Review* 22, no. 2 (July/August 1995).

"À la Recherche de la Poésie Perdue," *American Poetry Review* (forthcoming).

"Connoisseurs of Loneliness": section 1 appeared in *Denver Quarterly* 24, no. 4 (spring 1990); section 2 in *Field* 31 (fall 1984).

"A Solving Emptiness": section 1 (as "The Disparates Fuse") appeared in *Parnassus* 16, no. 1 (fall 1990); section 2 (as "*Zone Journals*") in *New Virginia Review* 8 (spring 1991); reprinted in *The Point Where All Things Meet: Essays on Charles Wright,* ed. Tom Andrews (Oberlin: Oberlin University Press, 1995).

"In a Glass, Darkly": as "Notes Toward a Defense of Contemporary Poetry," *New England Review* 8, no. 3 (spring 1986).

A Poetry of Two Minds

A Toy Balloon,
the Man-Moth's Tear,
and a Sack of
Ripe Tomatoes

~~~~~

Poetry, Reticence,
and Attention

Although his prose typically maintains an effortless balance between the poetic and philosophic, J. D. Salinger resists being thought of as a poet or a philosopher. Still, he has created as his exemplary fictional character (if not his most endearing one, an honor reserved for that perennial star, Holden Caulfield) a man who is both: the loveable, tragic, enlightened figure of Seymour Glass. And Seymour Glass incidentally provides the clearest glimpse into the poetic ideas of his creator, for as his devoted brother Buddy none-too-shyly observes, Seymour is "a true poet."

One doesn't expect a fiction writer to do all the things his characters can; and, as is often the case with fictional poets, Seymour's poetry surfaces not in the form of poems, but in the occasional anecdote which conveys some feel for the poetic sensibility behind them. Here's one example, told by Buddy, which I offer with all the trumpeted fanfare to which the station of "true poet" is entitled:

> [One of Seymour's poems] is about a young married woman and mother who is plainly having what it refers to here in my old marriage manual as an extramarital love affair. Seymour doesn't describe

her, but she comes into the poem just when that cornet of his is doing something extraordinarily effective, and I see her as a terribly pretty girl, moderately intelligent, immoderately unhappy, and not unlikely living a block or two away from the Metropolitan Museum of Art. She comes home very late one night from a tryst—in my mind, bleary and lipstick smeared—to find a balloon on her bedspread. Someone has simply left it there. The poet doesn't say, but it can't be anything but a large, inflated toy balloon, probably green, like Central Park in spring.[1]

In discussing a poem by Elizabeth Bishop, Randall Jarrell once observed that poetry, the best poetry anyway, communicates by a kind of reticence, by something the poem *doesn't* say that a reader still somehow manages to get. Reticence may seem a modest goal for a poet, especially at a time when poets appear, more often than not, inclined toward disclosure and explicitness. Nevertheless I want to explore, through the allegorical model of Buddy's story, the supple paradox of Jarrell's remark. I want to see how far we can go in pursuing what it is a poem withholds or cloisters within its language. Moreover, I want to consider the no less mystifying sleight-of-hand by which a poem imparts the experience of that withholding. (But why turn, one might ask, to a fictional character's second-hand account of a nonexistent poem by a poet almost too good to be true? My only answer: Years of reading Salinger has taught me, among other things, that poetry tends to present itself in the most unlikely places, in the most unlikely forms.)

To frame these comments in the context of Buddy's narrative: How is it that something as unrelated as the toy balloon the adulterous woman finds floating on her bed still manages to convey the full weight and perplexity of her sorrow? And how is it that the balloon becomes so clearly realized in Buddy's mind when he's already told us that "the poet doesn't say" anything about the balloon itself? For all its breezy delivery, this passage provides a surprisingly acute tutorial in the process by which the words on a page get transformed into mental (that is, nonverbal) images in the mind of the reader.

Let's look more closely: "The poet doesn't say, but it can't be anything but a large, inflated toy balloon, probably green, like Central Park in spring." Apparently, much of what gets expressed by the poem is expressed without its words; at the same time, Buddy is careful to separate this fact from the old cliché, and the born again theory, that poems are open to whatever meanings a reader chooses to impose on them: "The poet doesn't say, but *it can't be anything but. . . .*"

At this point in Buddy's narrative, things get curiouser and curiouser. It appears that through the subtle alchemy of Seymour's words, the poem lifts off the sturdy branch of the written page and settles in the mind of the reader. And there it begins to acquire detail not present in the poem at all: "The poet doesn't say, but it can't be anything but a large, inflated toy balloon, probably green." For most mortal poets that accomplishment alone would suffice, and we'd be right to greet it with a round of applause. But for this particular poet wonder is never an end in itself. Not only has the poem managed, by a kind of reticence, to convey the size, shape, kind, and color of the balloon, it has also conveyed something the text never mentions. For Buddy now imagines that the color of the balloon is "green, like Central Park in spring," a comparison that comes, not from the poet's words, but from the reader's (Buddy's) imagination. In what seems to me poetry's most sublime effect, the poem confers on its fortunate reader the very same act of imagination which gave rise to the poem in the first place. Just as another Salinger character once famously offered up one half of his chicken-salad sandwich, the poem offers up its inspiration, offers to make the reader the poet.

◆

From *reticence* to *communication* to *inspiration*—that's a fairly long road to travel in the course of one small (and imaginary) poem. But it's just such roads that lead us to pursue the poetic ideas of this writer. As everyone knows, Salinger's work has enjoyed great, if unwanted, success since *Catcher in the Rye*, and his decidedly cranky taste in poetry is well-documented by now: he maintains a strong dislike for T. S. Eliot—all that academese, as Franny so firmly but politely points out in *Franny and Zooey*—and he holds in almost religious awe both Sappho and Rainer Maria Rilke.

Franny, it turns out, is especially fond of the Sappho we encounter in the following fragment:

> Delicate Adonis is dying, Cythera,
> what shall we do?
> Beat your breasts, maidens,
> and rend your tunics.

Through the course of the novel it becomes increasingly clear that what Franny loves in this fragment is its largely *unspoken* directness. At the simplest level, Sappho's poem poses a question: In the face of dying, what can we do? And Cythera appears to have an answer, an answer both immediate and practical: You can mourn, "Beat your breasts, maidens, / and rend your tunics." The poem's authority derives in part from the dizzying swiftness with which it comes to significance: In the face of dying, mourning is what, perhaps all, we can do—but mourning is not nothing. It's a way we have to make use of our sorrow, to form a sympathetic bond with the dying, and, in the face of that otherwise paralyzing question ("What can we do?"), to form an adequate response. By the charged expressive reticence of those lines, we discover through an inroad to the human heart the enabling truth of their meanings.

◆

It's a Romantic notion that poets have access to some special or higher kind of meaning, and we're right to be skeptical of all such claims. But poets are saved from the lie and preserved in the truth of that notion since their meanings are carried in the effects of their words and not in their concepts. And since words are less mutable than ideas, what endures in a poem is a privilege of its language (as pleasure, not signification), just as what endures in music is a privilege of its sounds (as pleasure, not signification). Still, the attribute I'm trying to isolate is not simply one of language, for language is really the outcome, and, as such, it's preceded by perception, and perception by intuition, and intuition by something else.

The quality I'm after resides somewhere in that "something else," in that pre-reflective consciousness which serves as the wellspring of intuition, perception, and poetry. I'm referring not to that ghost-haunted storehouse we call the subconscious, but to that heightened wakefulness we call "attention." And in poetry, it seems, everything begins with attention, with that alertness which Walter Benjamin called "the natural prayer of the soul."

Perhaps attention is one instinctual gauge by which we measure a poem's effectiveness: the act of concentration that reveals to us (groundlings of ordinary perception) things not available otherwise. It's that same wide-eyed receptivity we encounter so often in Marianne Moore, in such moments as when she happens to observe, while watching a mockingbird return to feed, "three / large fledgling[s] . . . below / the pussy-willow tree":

> Toward the high-keyed intermittent squeak
>   of broken carriage springs, made by
> the three similar, meek-
>   coated bird's-eye
> freckled forms she comes; and when
> from the beak
>   of one, the still living
>   beetle has dropped
> out, she picks it up and puts
> it in again. ("Bird-Witted")

Or when Elizabeth Bishop, her attention turned to the wholly imaginary figure of a "man-moth," details her subject with the fine articulations of a lepidopterist's pen:

>   If you catch him,
> hold up a flashlight to his eye. It's all dark pupil,
> an entire night itself, whose haired horizon tightens

as he stares back, and closes up the eye. Then from the lids
one tear, his only possession, like the bee's sting, slips.
Slyly he palms it, and if you're not paying attention
he'll swallow it. However, if you watch, he'll hand it over,
cool as from underground springs and pure enough to drink.
   ("The Man-Moth")

In the poignant apposition of those last three lines, Bishop discloses
the secret resource of her art: the "clear," "pure" gift that is handed
over to those who dare pay attention.

    ♦

The uses of attention require special notice in an age like ours, when
the senses (the way we pay attention) are being bombarded at a rate
unprecedented in the history of the world; and when the world as
we've known it through the senses is being rapidly and continually
revised. This was a danger Cézanne anticipated even as the twentieth
century began: "Things are in a bad way. We shall have to hurry if
we want to see anything. Everything is vanishing." In the face of such
vanishings, it's no wonder we feel that something has come between
us and the world, no wonder we've seen the arts in our age grow more
and more inward and insular. For inevitably the eye turns in on itself,
and the self thereby becomes our one accessible subject.

    This is a concern Salinger appears to share, especially as regards
the poet. Except for Sappho and Rilke his preferences in poetry tend
toward Chinese and Japanese classical verses, and for the following
reason: "For the most part I'd say that unless a Chinese or Japanese
poet's real forte is knowing a good persimmon or a good crab or a
good mosquito bite on a good arm when he sees one, then no matter how long or unusual or fascinating his semantic or intellectual in-
testines may be, or how beguiling they sound . . . no one . . . speaks
seriously of him as a poet." The serious poet, in other words, is one
whose attentions are tuned, not to the lone frequency of the self's vi-
brations, but to the myriad bands that gather to compose the elusive
flux of daily life.

    So how does one come to recognize a good persimmon or a good crab or a good mosquito bite on a good arm? One can be sure that, in his characteristic way, Salinger has secreted a story or two that will help us formulate an answer. This one I discovered in *Seymour—An Introduction*, and the narrator, again, is Seymour's brother Buddy:

> Once, a terrible number of years ago, when Seymour and I were eight and six, our parents gave a party for nearly sixty people in our three and a half rooms at the old Hotel Alamac, in New York. They were officially retiring from vaudeville, and it was an affecting as well as celebrative occasion. We two were allowed to get out of bed around eleven or so, and come in and have a look. We had more than a look. . . . We danced, we sang, first singly, then together. . . . But mostly we just stayed up and watched. Toward two in the morning, when the leave-takings began, Seymour begged Bessie—our mother—to let him bring the leavers their coats. . . . He and I knew about a dozen of the guests intimately, ten or so more by sight or reputation, and the rest not at all or hardly. We had been in bed, I should add, when everyone arrived. But from watching the guests for some three hours, from grinning at them, from, I think, loving them, Seymour—without asking any questions first—brought very nearly all the guests, one or two at a time, and without any mistakes, their own true coats, and all the men involved their hats.[2]

There is much to be learned from this passage, and it deserves its own accounting; but what interests me most is what, without saying it, it says about poetry. For this is no ordinary observation Seymour has performed, but a kind that resembles the openness, sympathy and receptivity which Keats set aside as distinguishing qualities of the poet. In a scene reminiscent of the Glass family party, Keats in one of his letters describes the selflessness that follows this state of mind: "When I am in a room with People if I ever am free from speculating on creations of my own brain, then not myself goes home to myself: but the identity of every one in the room begins to press upon me."

"From *watching* the guests . . . from *grinning* at them, from, I think, *loving* them . . ." It may be worth considering these endeavors as requisite features of poetic composition; and it may be worth considering them, in a very literal sense, as activities. As Salinger would later observe, poetry "is a crisis, perhaps the only actionable one we can call our own."

It would seem, then, that our first responsibility, once we've come face-to-face with our subject, is to push beyond those elements we *already recognize,* those elements that normally serve as both the end and limit of our knowing. It is said that Rembrandt, in painting a portrait, would force himself to paint the same head repeatedly, that only then was he able to get to its *unfamiliarity,* its raw truth. And to do that meant pushing beyond his own perceptions, for familiarity is a condition, not within the one observed, but within the one observing. For Keats this required nothing less than the extinction of the ego, so that the "poetical Character," as he called it, becomes both "characterless" and "camelion"-like; that is, "it has no self—it is everything and nothing."

In Keats's mind, this openness—which he famously calls "Negative Capability"—occurs when one engages one's subject "without any irritable reaching after fact & reason." Perhaps this explains why, "without asking any questions first," Seymour managed to bring "nearly all the guests, one or two at a time, and without any mistakes, their own true coats, and all the men involved their hats." This particular form of imaginative intelligence Keats called "the sense of Beauty," and he passionately held to its standard: "The sense of Beauty overcomes every other consideration, or rather obliterates all consideration."

◆

The preceding remarks might lead one to believe that I consider these issues an exclusive concern of poetry, and poetry an exclusive concern of poets. That's not the case. And to counter that impression I'd like to propose a slightly broader application of the terms.

Several months ago, on a weekend evening in the early fall, my wife and I and another couple went over to a friend's house for dinner. Our friend, a recently divorced grade-school teacher, Annie, greeted us at the side door with her eight-year-old son, Michael. We sat outside and talked for a while, and, when time came to go in for dinner, Michael grabbed a sandwich and left the adults to their meal. The plates were just being served—large platters of bread, cheeses, and home-grown vegetables—when the telephone rang and Annie left to answer. A few minutes later she returned, visibly shaken, and took her seat at the table. Someone asked if she was okay, and in a voice tremulous with emotion, she explained that the woman who lived next door had called to say her husband had just been taken to the hospital. They were an older couple, Annie told us, and he hadn't been well for some time.

The meal laid out so sumptuously before us now seemed a mild reproach, and Annie made a brave, unsuccessful attempt to restore its former glow. There we sat, faced with that question Sappho had posed: "Delicate Adonis is dying, Cythera, what shall we do?" And Annie, like Cythera, quickly came to an answer, an answer both immediate and practical. Pushing back from the table, she excused herself and went outside to the garden. And when she came back in she was carrying an armful of tomatoes, "the last tomatoes of the season," she said. She then put the tomatoes in a paper sack and called to Michael, who'd been upstairs playing when the telephone rang. She asked him to go next door and leave the sack on the neighbors' back steps, but not to knock on their door, not to disturb them.

Apparently Michael was used to having free run of both houses, for he greeted this request with a furrowed brow. "What's the matter? How come I can't knock on the door?" As parents will, Annie explained that the neighbors were busy and not to be bothered. But the tone in her voice belied her explanation, and the boy departed without further question.

An hour or two later, the dishes done, my wife and I made our good-byes. The two houses shared a common driveway, and walking to the car I noticed that, on the neighbors' back steps, Michael had lined up in order of size, from the largest to the smallest, from the first step to the landing, those five ripe tomatoes. And though I can't be sure, I had the impression that each of those tomatoes had been polished very carefully on a sleeve.

If one accepts Keats's belief that the poet is less an identity than a responsive sensibility, then one could say that Michael possessed, to whatever small or large degree, a similarly responsive nature. Not only had he seen through his mother's sad attempt to shelter him from their neighbors' misfortune, but he'd also managed, "without asking any questions first," to turn this perception into an active form of sympathy. A sympathy which found expression in the polished arrangement on the back steps of their neighbor's house. And is it going too far to suggest that those five tomatoes lined up that way, largest to smallest, one on each step, constituted a kind of poetic form? And that, however unsophisticated a form it was, it nonetheless constituted an aesthetic structure arrived at by that very same process Seymour had employed on the night of his parents' party?

The general accessibility of these intuitions locates poetry, in my opinion, right where it belongs, in the "holiness of the heart's affections," as Keats described it, "and the truth of imagination." And if that's the place where poetry finds its reason for being, it's also a place that serves us all as a forcing house for human understanding. Whether poetry will be able to sustain this purpose through the myriad refusals and recombinations our fin-de-siècle necessarily entails is still in question. One only hopes that, in coming to an answer, we will give it our most serious attention.

On the Memory
of Stone

A Jeffers Legacy

In 1996 the board members of the Robinson Jeffers Tor House Foundation kindly invited me to make a few remarks about the experience of living for several years, from high school on, in general proximity of the house and tower which Jeffers built at the tip of Carmel Point. Tor House is located about a hundred miles south of San Francisco, about forty miles north of Big Sur, a location reflective of a lifelong division in Jeffers's mind: the massive encroachments of civilization on one side, the raw, unsettled wilderness on the other.

Given the period I lived there, a period in which certain key if unconscious decisions were made about the shape my future life would take, my remarks inevitably took into account the influence Jeffers's presence had on my decision to become a poet. Or at least on my decision to consider poetry something to which a man might meaningfully devote himself. For to paraphrase Patrick Kavanagh, a boy once fiddled around with verses and discovered they were his life.

Though it's one of poetry's universal charms to make each thoughtful reader feel a special self-enfolding grace, a secret power of exclusiveness—as if the words were written for our ears alone—poets read other poets, I've noticed, with even more self-interest than the average reader. For the poet/reader those words may do more than simply touch the wellsprings of your inmost life; they may also contain (for such is the nature of self-interest) some message encoded just for you, some personal clue to the workings of this art. Like Virgil's hand, those words may lend a much-needed guidance in finding your way past the spiraling emptiness of the next blank page. And in ways I wouldn't realize for years, Jeffers had offered that hand.

♦

After years of a rather nomadic life in the military, my family finally settled, in 1965, in a hillside house a mile or so from that wide horseshoe-inlet where the Carmel River empties into the sea. Normally the river runs dry by late spring, and it's an easy thirty-minute walk from where we lived to reach the other side. To this day I can recreate, step by step, that walk in my mind: the scent of wild sage and drying kelp, the flare of Indian paintbrush, the dusty footpath through ice-plant and sea grass that followed up over a treeless hill and down an embankment on the northern side. From there I'd cross, shoes in hand, the gaping mouth of the riverbed, then continue along the beach below that legendary house where a poet named Robinson Jeffers died three years before.

I took this walk often, almost daily in the summers—it was the shortest route by foot into town—and not always but sometimes I'd circle behind the poet's house and pause outside its wooden gate. I must've done this more noticeably than I realized, for one day a courteous, middle-aged man stepped from the house and asked what I was doing. I told him I can't remember what—perhaps that we were "neighbors"?—but whatever it was it was apparently enough to keep him from chasing me off.

In fact, to my still retrievable wonder, he explained how he didn't really have much time, but perhaps I'd like a quick look inside. I would indeed. He introduced himself as Donnan Jeffers, one of the poet's twin sons, and without further ceremony he led me into the interior—an interior as allegorical as it was austere, as anachronistic as it was novel, as rife with psychological mystery as it was bone-bound, elemental, and enclosed. Is this, I wondered, what the poets' world is truly like? Is this their natural element? Clearly, I was in way over my boyish head, and while I can't say that my life was "changed," I can say that the house and tower had a homeopathic effect on me, a regional de-centering that lingered for years to come, and took forms I could not have foreseen.

♦

My father, whose family was third-generation northern Californian, had remembered Carmel from his childhood days as one of those utopian artist communities that appear in California from time to time. My mother is a painter who was raised in the south, and I suspect my father had that in mind—Carmel's family of artisans, its incomparable stretch of seacoast—when he took us there to settle. I was fifteen when we arrived, and, having spent most of my life either on or around military bases, Carmel felt rather alien to me, cultivated and rich and societal. And given how much its character had changed since that formative community of artists, my parents must've found it odd as well. I hadn't known about Jeffers then—in fact, the first "local writer" I read with interest was Henry Miller, who lived a half hour's drive down the coast—and poetry was something I imagined being written by a species unlike my own. But I soon came to hear about the Jeffers house, the stone embodiment of the Jeffers myth, and the name had already formed itself as a remotely beckoning island in the mind.

As fate would have it, one afternoon while I was visiting a friend it came up in conversation that his grandfather had been a photographer. We were sitting, as I recall, in his well-lit kitchen when he opened a drawer and took out a folder of the Johan Hagemeyer portraits of Una and Robinson Jeffers. I'm not sure why they affected me so, but that proud, raw-boned man and woman awakened a deep curiosity in me, a curiosity about what I took to be the secret history, the buried nature, of that place picturesquely referred to as Carmel-by-the-Sea. It was as if the portraits had summoned from a deeper level of consciousness what lay below the surface of that storybook town; as if the town itself was infused with that spirit. Whatever the case, from that day on I observed my newly-adopted home through a different and clearly wider lens. Moreover, I sensed this mysterious "other life" had something to do with poetry, with the measure of the world that poems must take, and with a poet named Robinson Jeffers.

It wasn't until some time later, when I'd enrolled at the nearby junior college, that I began in earnest and on my own to read through Jeffers's poems. As it turned out, my reading happened to coincide with that period when I'd begun "composing" those first heartfelt utterances I blushingly referred to as "verses." But despite the no-doubt burning passions with which I invested those pages, I suspect my enthusiasm had less to do with the poems I was writing than the poet I was reading. For now, these many years later, I realize that what I needed at the time was a poet who would, not mirror my own mind (for at that age I could hardly pretend to possess one), but make real for me a notion of sensibility durable enough to sustain the interests of my own wildly undirected yearnings.

❖

I came to Jeffers long before I knew anything about his (or anyone's) "literary standing." Still, it didn't take long to discover that, within the American literary establishment, and within the American academy as well, Jeffers was something of an outcast, an unfashionable exception to the deeply entrenched precepts of modernism. Even now, despite my impression that he's largely undervalued, I tend to see him, and see him by nature, as somehow existing outside all that—a willful, iconoclastic, defiant solitaire. When it came down to it, I told myself, one could no more rank Robinson Jeffers than one could rank a storm-wracked cypress tree. It seemed to me then, and it seems to me still, that his appeal is genuinely unique in that way. Here is a poet, rare in a century so often defined by the prototypical obscurities of *The Waste Land*, who makes one feel more interested in learning from him than in learning about him. Moreover, the established protocols of connoisseurship that so tightly surround the literary world seemed another symptom of that social intrusion this poet had warned would take the wild out of the wilderness.

For that reason more than any other, I believe my early infatuation with Jeffers was extremely lucky for me. Lucky because it turned me away from the insular fascinations of literary affairs, and turned me back to what one demonstrative poem has called "This wild swan of a world" ("Love the Wild Swan"), the raw physical reality around us. And for someone meekly preparing to engage that long blank stare which poets in this country are likely to arouse, it was useful to admire a poet who possessed the audacity to claim, as Jeffers had done, that serious poets should shun the "doctrinaire corruptions of instinct" which drive lesser writers to seek out the petty consolations of fame:

> To be peered at and interviewed, to be pursued by idlers and autograph hunters and inquiring admirers, would surely be a sad nuisance. And it is destructive too, if you take it seriously; it wastes your energy into self-consciousness; it destroys spontaneity and soils the springs of the mind. Whereas posthumous reputation could do you no harm at all, and is really the only kind worth considering. ("Poetry, Gongorism and a Thousand Years")

It was only much later that I began to feel there was something disingenuous in that lofty pose. Even famous poets aren't *that* famous, after all. And perhaps that tone of worldly indifference concealed more heartbreak than it dared let on. At the time of its writing, Jeffers was already disappearing from the standard anthologies of American literature, and by the time of his death he was virtually forgotten. Furthermore, a poet so confident in the ultimate value of what he does—as Jeffers often noted in the example of Yeats—could hardly be distracted by the passing notice of the small, at best, poetry public. As is frequently the case, a ferocious self-assurance seemed to mask an equally ferocious self-doubt.

Still, for a young poet facing the glum prospect of a growing stack of rejection slips, such lessons were useful in a number of ways, and for a number of reasons. Not only did they encourage me to seek an essential faith in the work *as work*, independent of its relative value, but they also provided a means of explaining to friends and family alike that my poems spoke to posterity, however little they did to them. And that one sure sign of their timelessness was the fact that they managed so successfully to keep at bay those idle packs of "autograph hunters and inquiring admirers."

And so it was, in my happy self-delusions, that I began sketching out some shadowy, half-formed likeness of "the poet," a likeness that was probably equal parts my own invention and the man named Robinson Jeffers. For in my mind, the virtues of this poet were as yet untempered by his excesses: by that tone of valediction which rolls so easily off his tongue; by his periodic sage-struck posturing; by his categorical view of human history, his pulpit speeches and deadpan prose; by his demonized vision of mass society and modern industrialization.

For the moment anyway, my Jeffers was positioned above all that, and a nobler spirit was still to be found in yet another portrait, by yet another remarkable Carmel photographer, Edward Weston. In Weston's photograph the instinct was rife and brought sharply into focus by a mildly bohemian flyaway collar; by the black Irish features weathered to a look "indigenous" to the central California coast; and by a deep-set gaze that derived its knowledge from the darker realms, a gaze that kept its secrets.

◆

By his own account Jeffers was "cold and undiscriminating" by nature, though perhaps it's really more accurate to say that he was cold and undiscriminating *like* nature. The springs of his genius seemed to well up from a connection to the primitive sources of life; and out of those sources his imagination formed two great and anachronistic powers, powers that have rarely come together in any other poet in this century: a profound kinship with the blood-wrought Hellenistic spirit through which he infused Christian symbology with a fearsome pagan energy; and the resolve to bring back to a secular culture the fierce Old Testament character of the spiritual life. At their most fevered pitch, his poems can sound less spoken from the page than broadcast like oracles from the crumbling sea cliffs of the Western world.

Needless to say, Jeffers's work proved a pretty strong brew for a boy in his teens, and I confess that there was something in him which frightened me. This was, after all, the poet who'd once unflinchingly claimed, "I'd sooner, except the penalties, kill a man than a hawk," then coolly dispatched a wounded red-tail: "I gave him the lead gift in the twilight" ("Hurt Hawks"). The poet who'd broached the taboo worlds of incest, blood lust, bestiality, and revenge. The poet who'd once instructed his sons to take to the mountains when humanity arrived. The poet who'd made us step back to see the glutted body of civilization lumbering toward self-destruction. At every turn of the page, it seemed, death was nearby waiting in the wings, ready in an instant to claim the stage.

But if something in Jeffers frightened me, something had also awakened a feel for the stirring physical robustness, the rough materiality that's possible in a poem. Like some character out of Greek tragedy, he projected a powerful sense of living on the brink of a great disaster, and of having come face to face with the leveling forces behind it. First and foremost he was a moralist, a moralist of anger and outrage, of self-reliance and apostasy, a poet of grand apocalyptic gestures who drew his authority from the earth and sea. His poems could make one shudder to think the almost unthinkable thought: the more inhuman, the more divine. He was as bleak and unremitting as Thomas Hardy, as divinely inspired as Walt Whitman, and he spoke in an ancient, Job-like voice that sounded from the headlong opening lines of the six hundred pages of his *Selected Poetry:*

A night the half-moon was like a dancing-girl,
No, like a drunkard's last half-dollar
Shoved on the polished bar of the eastern hill-range,
Young Cauldwell rode his pony along the sea-cliff;
When she stopped, spurred; when she trembled, drove

The teeth of the little jagged wheels so deep
They tasted blood; the mare with four slim hooves
On a foot of ground pivoted like a top,
Jumped from the crumble of sod, went down, caught, slipped;
Then, the quick frenzy finished, stiffening herself
Slid with her drunken rider down the ledges,
Shot from sheer rock and broke
Her life out on the rounded tidal boulders. ("Tamar")

Perhaps you can imagine the dizzying effect this passage might've had on a boy who, until then, had always assumed that poetry derived from the fine sensations, the sensitive soul. A boy who'd probably felt right at home with the loveliness of that opening line, only to have it contravened by the preemptive strike of the second.

And who, I wondered, had uttered that sharp corrective "no"? Who, in a word, had canceled the strict decorums of literature and set in their place this cruder, more urgent, more pressing reality? Who, in a word, had proclaimed straight off that poetry resides, not in the delicate phrasings of a "half-moon . . . like a dancing-girl," but in the rough, staged accents of verse narrative? Rightly or wrongly—and certainly obscurely—I linked this "no" to what Jeffers himself, in the abbreviated foreword two pages earlier, had directed at literary modernism:

> Long ago, before anything included here was written, it became evident to me that poetry—if it was to survive at all—must reclaim some of the power and reality that it was so hastily surrendering to prose. The modern French poetry of that time, and the most "modern" of the English poetry, seemed to me thoroughly defeatist, as if poetry were in terror of prose, and desperately trying to save its soul from the victor by giving up its body. It was becoming slight and fantastic, abstract, unreal, eccentric; and was not even saving its soul, for these are generally anti-poetic qualities. It must reclaim substance and sense, and physical and psychological reality. . . . It was not in

my mind to open new fields for poetry, but only to reclaim an old freedom.

In the stanza quoted above, one could see what Jeffers meant by poetry's "body," by "substance and sense, and physical and psychological reality." It is there in the tortured figure of the pony, an animal charged with a sublimated sexual agony driven by the brute directives of her rider: "When she stopped, spurred; when she trembled, drove / The teeth of the little jagged wheels so deep / They tasted blood." And this is followed by a terrible fall as the pony, "stiffening herself / Slid with her drunken rider down the ledges, / Shot from sheer rock and broke / Her life out on the rounded tidal boulders." (For years I misread that final line, changing "tidal" to "bridal," thereby cinching a three-part linkage between sex and violence and nature, a misreading, it amuses me to think, that Jeffers might well have foreseen.)

In the thirteen lines of that opening sentence, the sentence which launches the epic and masterful narrative "Tamar," Jeffers set out to reclaim an "old freedom," the freedom of the story. In his mind it was only through narrative that literature could reclaim its historical relationship to the temporal world. From Homer to the beginnings of the twentieth century, narrative remained the firm foundation, the enduring cornerstone of the Western world's greatest literature. His was the first century to call that tradition into question, and every instinctual bone in Jeffers registered that departure as a decadence. If the laudable determination of his revolt would prove a limitation in his poems, that would happen by design, not accident:

Prose can discuss matters of the moment; poetry must deal with things that a reader two thousand years away could understand and be moved by. This excludes much of the circumstance of modern life, especially in the cities. Fashions, forms of machinery, the more complex social, financial, political adjustments, and so forth, are all ephemeral, exceptional; they exist but will never exist again. Poetry must concern itself with (relatively) permanent things. These have poetic value; the ephemeral has only news value.[1]

The idea of someone advocating a poetry which "excludes much of the circumstances of modern life, especially in the cities," sounds naive to us today, dangerously out of synch with the historical and literary imperatives of our time. And except for Jeffers, it's hard to think of a single twentieth-century poet who would welcome that description. For better or worse, his vision was cosmic in extent, singular in purpose; and as his own "Post Mortem" informs us, it showed little interest in the passing activities of the daily world, that "exuberance" which will, in any case,

> canker and fall in its time and like
> clouds the houses
> Unframe, the granite of the prime
> Stand from the heaps: come storm and wash clean:
> the plaster is all run to the sea and the steel
> All rusted; the foreland resumes
> The form we loved when we saw it.

♦

A final point I would make about Jeffers concerns his interest in stone, one half of his celebrated twin deities, the other being the hawk. Jeffers's readers are, if anything, overly familiar with this interest, though I sometimes feel that our familiarity has kept us from fully tapping its mystery. We tend to overlook how consuming an interest it was, and how dramatically it embodies the thematic preoccupations of his life and work. Perhaps not since Wordsworth has a poet placed such high regard on such a lowly form, or culled from a pile of "unhewn stones" such a legible record of human history.

Donnan Jeffers, the poet's son, has written a curious little monograph, "The Stones of Tor House," a brief descriptive catalog of indigenous and exotic stones still to be found on the property. In addition to boulders pulleyed and levered up from the beach below to construct the house and tower, the collection includes pieces gathered from sites all over the world: a small gray pebble from the top of Croagh Patrick, the holy mountain in Ireland; another from the Caves of Nerja in Spain; a chunk of obsidian from Glass Mountain, California; a piece of Hawaiian lava; pebbles from the beach below "King Arthur's Castle" in Cornwall; a red and white "pudding stone" from the Michigan farm of Una's father; a pink stone flecked with mica from the banks of the Oka river in Russia. . . . The list goes on and on.[2]

I was reminded of all this recently, when one of the Tor House docents took me back through the property for the first time since my visit there nearly thirty years before. What sort of person, I now found myself asking, what sort of person not only builds a house and tower of stone but has mortared into the retaining walls, footpaths, lintels, and chimneys, over doorways and fireplaces, inside and out, countless stones collected on travels all over the globe?[3] And what underlay the explicit connection he'd drawn, on any number of occasions, between a stone and a poem?

To the degree that one can formulate an answer based on Jeffers's poems, one might reasonably argue that, like poetry, stones contain a manifold unspoken history and a sacral connection to their native soil. Like poetry, one engages them first as substance, color, texture, form, as objects of sensory investigation. And like poetry, their meaning resides *inside*, in that living invisible presence Jeffers called a "massive / Mysticism," a "fate going on / Outside our fates."[4] In that sense, they are, or they lead us to feel, the incarnation not of history alone, but of the fundamental experience of time.

If I'm not making too much of this, it might be said that in Jeffers's cosmology stone is infused with the great, abiding spirit of the past. Not only does stone contain the *prehistoric* time of the earth's formation, the *geologic* time of the stone itself, the *geographic* time of the stone's location, and the *historic* time of its cultural surrounds, but the person who bends to pick one up adds to it the *personal time* of his or her own life.

Time, Jeffers knew, is written in stone, and a pebble in his pocket was like a seed carried off on the feathers of a bird, or the tusk of a wooly mammoth conveyed by glacier down a riverbed. It was his way of adding time to time, memory to memory, like water poured into water. We can imagine such scenes played out repeatedly in Jeffers's life: On a warm spring evening in Galway, he and Una take a walk together around the tower that once belonged to Yeats. In the uncut grass beside the tower, Una discovers a charred, palm-sized piece of stone (the slag from a coal fire?) and puts it in her pocket. And through that gesture a chord is sounded in the circle of time: Una and Robin are connected to a poet named Yeats, Yeats is connected to Irish history, Irish history to its ancient Celtic traditions, those traditions to the soil from which was drawn the very same coal that Yeats (perhaps) had burned down to a scrap of slag. And then of course those of us who, mindfully or not, have come to touch, in the Tor House gardens, that piece of slag mortared between two paving stones, we too are added to its ever deepening inner life.

In Jeffers's mind stones were living things, "grave, earnest, not passive" (606). For him they served as the repositories of memory, objects of a deep residual value replete with a past and possessed of an unarticulated history that far outreaches those momentary tracings we call our own. And they're distinguished (favorably) from human nature by their "dark peace," their "final disinterestedness" (563), their "stone endurance" (83).

By seeing them this way, Jeffers establishes a relationship to the natural world that's no longer based on a subject speaking to an object (whereby the human holds priority and the natural world becomes raw material) but on a subject speaking to a subject (whereby the natural world requires reciprocal care). Is it any wonder, then, that before laying the cornerstone for his house the poet would prepare a heady offering of "Wine and white milk and honey"?

> I did not dream the taste of wine could bind with granite,
> Nor honey and milk please you; but sweetly
> They mingle down the storm-worn cracks among the mosses,

Interpenetrating the silent
Wing-prints of ancient weathers long at peace, and the older
Scars of primal fire, and the stone
Endurance that is waiting millions of years to carry
A corner of the house, this also destined. ("To the Rock That Will
    Be a Cornerstone of the House")

In Celtic mythology there exists the belief that the souls of the
dead inhabit inanimate objects, and that the soul remains within that
object until, by touching it, someone passing releases the spirit back
to the air. Within the stone walls of the Jeffers house we feel the
truth that lies behind that powerful fiction. And if poetry is, as
Jeffers maintains, "sometimes harder than granite" ("Harder Than
Granite"), then stone and poem are equally places where the shade of
Jeffers might long survive the comings and goings of the daily world,
the fickle vacillations of literary fashion, the development of his
beloved wilderness. And in ten thousand years, should we in our idle-
ness return to his house, we needn't look further for his ghost:

                                            it is probably
Here, but a dark one, deep in the granite, not dancing on wind
With the mad wings and the day moon. ("Tor House")

A Story of
Poetry and Poets

Orpheus
and Eurydice

A man and a woman have fallen in love. On the day of their wedding the woman dies and is led away into the land of the shades. Against all the stern counsel of the upper world, and armed only with the mournful power of his song, the man attempts what no other mortal has ever dared: to pursue his beloved into the deepest reaches of the underworld.

And so begins the story of Orpheus and Eurydice, Western literature's formative myth of poetry and poets, a story whose characters set in motion a chain of events that come to suggest certain arcane truths which lie at the heart of poetry's art. At the crucial, decisive moments of its drama, this story looks inward on its own creators, and that painful self-reflexiveness reminds us of the twofold nature of those truths. Most particularly, it brings to light poetry's deep-seated link to love and death and the erotic; but also, and no less significantly, it reveals how poetry is as much concerned with what it chooses to keep secret (and what secrets it chooses to safeguard) as with what it chooses to disclose.

In either case secrecy is exposed as paramount to both the affective and substantive elements of this art—to its transportive sounds and its consistently elusive meanings. As the scholar Elizabeth Sewell has observed, "In the Orpheus story, myth is looking at itself. This is the reflection of myth in its own mirror. . . . Orpheus is poetry thinking about itself." [1]

♦

A man and a woman have fallen in love. On the day of their wedding the woman dies and is carried off into the underworld. For days following Eurydice's death, Orpheus mourns her loss in song. This, in itself, is already an unusual feature of the story. Traditionally the woman is the one who stays, the man the one who is taken away to some far-off place, some elsewhere. Traditionally, "it is Woman who gives shape to absence, elaborates its fiction," writes Roland Barthes in *A Lover's Discourse*, "for she has time to do so; she weaves and sings; the Spinning Songs express both immobility (by the hum of the Wheel) and absence (far away, rhythms of travel, sea surges, cavalcades)." [2] But here a man is left behind, a man who now gives shape to absence, a man who now elaborates the fiction of his loss. Orpheus himself must now express, through the Spinning Song of his powerful lyre, both immobility and absence.

"Man who waits and who suffers from his waiting is miraculously feminized." [3] Man who waits and who suffers from his waiting undergoes a change in nature. But Orpheus is also the one who desires— desires, perhaps, desire itself—a desire already making its way into the brooding melody of his lament. And here we might imagine: While listening in on his own song, a strange new thought occurs to the poet, and in that thought he suddenly experiences, like a fusion of terror and wonder, an emotion he has never experienced before. For a mortal has now conceived that he might roll back the very borders of death.

♦

A man and a woman have fallen in love. On the day of their marriage, almost as if the marriage itself had brought this on, the woman is bitten by a snake and dies. But this is no ordinary man. This is the supreme singer and patron of poetry, the son of Calliope—the "beautiful-voiced" Muse of epic poetry, one of the nine daughters of Mnemosyne, the goddess of memory—and, in varying accounts, of either a river-god, or King Oeagros of Thrace, or, more often, the sun-god Apollo, who presented him with a lyre.

Given this auspicious lineage, it's no wonder that Orpheus sang so sweetly that the fiercest warriors lay down their swords, wild beasts settled enthralled at his feet, even trees and stones uprooted themselves and drew up closer to hear. In a fifteenth-century drawing by the Italian artist Cima da Conegliano, a wan and melancholic Orpheus is pictured leaning against a tree, drawing a bow across his lyre, while deer, rabbits, and a mourning dove all gather around him to listen. In a later drawing by Cima, this very same head, in a similar attitude of sad repose, will serve to represent the biblical figure of Daniel; and like those creatures in the earlier drawing, a pair of lions have drawn up passively beside him, lulled by the presence of this mysterious man. Four centuries later, while composing his *Sonnets to Orpheus,* Rainer Maria Rilke would hang above his desk a print of Cima's *Orpheus;* and in Jean Cocteau's surrealist film *Orphée,* the café owner would remark to the poet who has entered his crowded literary club, "You have just come into the lions' den." It's as though, at each historical moment of the story, all the other moments are present.

◆

A man and a woman have fallen in love. On the day of their wedding, the woman dies and is led away into the underworld. After days of lamenting in the world above, the man decides he'll attempt to do what no other mortal has ever done, and what only a handful of the greatest heroes—men like Theseus, Odysseus, and Hercules—have ever even attempted: to rescue his beloved from the underworld.

Having crossed the river encircling Hades, having calmed the brutal, triple-throated dog who guards the gates to Taenarian, he comes face to face with Pluto and Persephone, the king and queen of the underworld. And then, caressing the strings of his sorrowful lyre, he intones his heartrending plea:

I wanted to be able
To bear this; I have tried to. . . .
    By these places
All full of fear, by this immense confusion,
By this vast kingdom's silences, I beg you,
Weave over Eurydice's life.[4]

Touched by the pathos of Orpheus's song, the surrounding phan-
toms, condemned for eternity to repeat their mindless sufferings—
Ixion bound to a fiery, winged, four-spoked wheel; the sun-parched
Tantalus reaching for water which recedes as he approaches; the vexed
king Sisyphus pushing his heavy stone uphill; and Tityos racked by
an endless pain as vultures feed off his liver—all are stilled in their
labors. As Ovid was moved to observe, "That was the first time ever
in all the world / The Furies wept."[5]

◆

That was the first time ever in all the world the Furies wept. Equally moved by
the mournful power of Orpheus's song, Pluto and Persephone summon Eurydice, still limping a little from her recent wound, to hear
them answer the poet. He may take her back to the upper world,
though only on one condition. A condition which, as some versions
have it, Persephone was first to declare: Until Orpheus has passed
through Avernus, through the gates that exit the domain of the dead,
he must not turn back to look on Eurydice.

It is the kind of condition, trivial on the surface, which at first
seems merely puzzling to the poet who has asked so much in return.
And yet it's the kind of condition—precisely because it was so trivial, and because it was linked to such a terrible cost—that the mind
of a poet would worry into larger significance. For Orpheus, "Eurydice is the limit of what art can attain; concealed behind a name
and covered by a veil, she is the profoundly dark point towards which
art, desire, death and the night all seem to lead." So says Maurice
Blanchot in "The Gaze of Orpheus."[6] And yet Orpheus is permitted
to do anything except approach this point face to face? Except see it

truly for what it is? Except possess that thing to which the whole of his being is drawn?

· •

Of Eurydice we know a good deal less than we do of Orpheus. Or do we? Perhaps predictably, given the strict patriarchal tradition from which this story derives, what we don't know about her is precisely what we do know: her mystery. For once she entered the underworld, that mystery became her identity, "the strangeness of that which excludes all intimacy."[7] Her name in Greek means "wide justice" and, tellingly, was originally thought to be a synonym for Persephone. A dryad, or oak-tree nymph, she was reputed to be a great beauty, like a glimpse of the gods or an exotic flower against the barren Thracian countryside. Many men longed for her, and on the day of her wedding, as she was walking with her companions through a nearby field, a passing shepherd attempted to carry her off. While fleeing her pursuer, Eurydice stepped on a poisonous snake and was instantly killed by its venom.

Curiously, at this point in the tale it's as though the name *Eurydice* begins to summon *someone else*. As though, once she descended into the underworld, she became *the other Eurydice*, one wrapped no longer "in her diurnal truth and her everyday charm, but in her nocturnal darkness, in her distance, her body closed, her face sealed."[8] And she became the repository for an apparently very powerful secret. A secret which Persephone's strict proscription seemed intent on trying to protect. It was as though, at the very moment the coiled snake struck, Eurydice recovered what Rilke calls "a new virginity" ("Orpheus. Eurydice. Hermes"), a virginity over which Persephone assumed a watchful, motherly charge. And what is the essence of virginity? Detachment. (*Copulation* means "mingling" with the world.) And what is the essence of detachment? Secrecy, mystery, and otherness.

By the eleventh line of Ovid's poem, Eurydice has become *the other Eurydice*, and in her new identity she has located herself outside the circle of Orpheus's knowledge. Orpheus's determination to pursue her derives from his inability to accept that loss—"I wanted to be able / To bear this; I have tried to."[9] But suppose this loss had already occurred, even before her death, in the very nature of love. As Barthes has observed (citing Winnicott): "The 'clinical fear of breakdown is the fear of a breakdown which has already been experienced (*primitive agony*). . . .' Similarly, it seems, for the lover's anxiety: it is the fear of a mourning which has already occurred, at the very origin of love, from the moment when I was first 'ravished.'"[10]

In dying, Eurydice is made strange. Orpheus, in attempting to bring her back, undertakes to make her familiar again. When Orpheus descends into the underworld, it's not to bring back the new Eurydice, it's to bring back the Eurydice he'd known before. Her capacity to love him the same way forever (is that what he secretly hoped to reclaim?) is predicated on her remaining the same woman who'd loved him originally. In order to go on loving him that way, she must remain familiar. Persephone's injunction—against the two of them standing face to face—is an injunction against that occurrence: You may not make her familiar again, you may not erase that original loss.

♦

That Eurydice's secret, the secret Persephone is determined to guard, may be linked to the erotic, perhaps even specifically to a female erotic, we may infer indirectly from another story, the story of a quarrel between Zeus and Hera about who derives the greater pleasure from sexual experience, a man or a woman. Unable to resolve this argument themselves, they call on the sage Tiresias, who answers their troubling question this way: If sexual pleasure could be divided into ten parts, a woman would have nine, a man only one. For revealing that secret, Tiresias is struck blind by Hera. But why? Because this was another of those secrets that poets and sages are called upon to safeguard. But why by Hera, one might ask, since she appears to have gained the advantage from his answer? Perhaps because, as Roberto Calasso speculates in *The Marriage of Cadmus and Harmony*, this is a secret which, once revealed, would confirm an already ancient fear that exists in men: "Perhaps woman, that creature shut away in the gynaeceum, where 'not a single particle of true eros penetrates,' knew a great deal more than her master." [11]

If, in dying, Eurydice became *the other Eurydice*, and if the nature of that otherness was detachment, then translated into the realm of the erotic this detachment denotes a certain independence from the phallus: "It wasn't so much love between women that scandalized the Greeks—to their credit they were not easily scandalized—as the suspicion, which had taken root in their minds, that women might have their own indecipherable erotic self-sufficiency." [12] And it may be that Persephone's prohibition against Orpheus gazing on Eurydice was founded on an awareness similar to that which engendered Hera's anger. The awareness that Eurydice possessed a secret—a secret apparently exposed in the dark of the underworld (the unconscious, where secrets are always exposed) but concealed in the light above (our waking lives, where repression, self-delusion, and avoidance reign)—a secret that must be protected from that ancient fear, hence from that potential wrath in men.

To see is to know. To know is to possess. To possess is to destroy. Such is the age-old cycle of seduction (in Greek, "to seduce" also means "to destroy"), and such is the fatal potential of the (male) gaze. Persephone, "the ice-cold queen," having been abducted by Pluto into the underworld, would know full well the power of men to overthrow a woman's will. To arrive, unexpected, and take possession. In her eyes, it may be that Orpheus has come, not to save Eurydice, but like so many gods and men before him, to abduct her into a world of his own. And what is the difference, after all?

◆

Having heard Persephone's proviso, Orpheus and Eurydice began to climb the narrowing path from the underworld. Up through the murk, through the chill, unbroken silence, up through the dark that clung like pitch to the rocky landscape around them. They had nearly arrived at that fateful border—Orpheus in the lead, Eurydice trailing safely behind—and they could just make out the dim light ahead, when a sudden foreboding (a *dementia*, in Virgil) took hold in

Orpheus. Was it the fear that she might falter? Some unchecked eagerness to see her again? The suspicion that he'd been tricked, after all, and it wasn't Eurydice who followed? Or had Eurydice, as in the Stravinsky-Balanchine ballet of the 1940s, conspired in her own death by calling to and caressing Orpheus as he attempted to leave the underworld? Whatever the case, the story explains that in a fatally impulsive gesture Orpheus turned and looked at her. And for one brief moment suspended in time, the two of them were indistinguishable: "Was it he, or she, reaching out arms and trying / To hold or to be held, and clasping nothing / But empty air." [13] For one brief moment they ceased to be either lover or beloved, subject or object, self or other; and in that moment their abjection was final and absolute.

◆

Most early Greek versions of the myth had Orpheus successfully rescuing Eurydice, and for medieval interpreters that happier, less ambiguous ending more accurately reflected the ideals of the Middle Ages. But ever since the Renaissance the Roman version has dominated literary and artistic interpretations. By elaborating the tragedy of Eurydice's second death, Virgil and Ovid shifted the emphasis from Orpheus's moral superiority to the romantic drama of the myth itself. For the modern reader, the details of that tragedy contain an inexhaustible mystery. Was this second death—because it was the second—even harder to bear than the first? Would Eurydice have been better off had Orpheus chosen not to come? Was this whole misadventure a foolish indulgence on Orpheus's part, an indulgence for which she must now pay a terrible price? In the deeply suggestive lines which conclude Ovid's account, Eurydice speaks the only word we hear from her: "She had no reproach to bring against her husband, / What was there to complain of? One thing, only: / He loved her. He could hardly hear her calling / *Farewell!* when she was gone." [14]

◆

Seen from one perspective, Eurydice serves a crucial role in the fate that Orpheus must undergo if he's to gain full powers as a poet. She comes to represent the descent into the poet's unconscious, the knowledge of the depths indispensable to artistic authority. As Hélène Cixous has observed, "We need a dead (wo)man to begin. To begin (writing, living) we must have death." [15]

Put another way, Eurydice must die (expiration) for Orpheus to claim the originative source (inspiration) of his not-yet-fully-realized song (suspiration). Oddly enough, this fate necessitates a proximity to, but not a possession of, those secrets that Eurydice embodies. That those secrets must remain secrets is evident not only in Persephone's injunction, but in the very fact that the ancient poets have so little to say about Eurydice. The Greek authors who mention her by name are relatively few, and it's largely from the Roman poets that we even learn of Orpheus's marriage. It's not until the Middle Ages that poets begin to give to her a more decisive voice in the story. And in the five hundred years that follow—as the tale is stripped of its traditional aura of mythic grandeur and recast in the context of ordinary lives—the psychological meanings begin to shift in profound and unforeseeable ways.

By the time the story reaches the twentieth century, the course of those meanings begins to come clear. In 1916 the American poet H. D. ventures to suggest that a woman might actually opt for a life in the underworld. Might choose instead of a "sheltered garden" (her phrase for the "borderline social case" of women, "not out of life, not in life") a less cultivated habitation all her own, a landscape which, by virtue of its remove from the domestic world, could awaken the slumbering female soul: "O to blot out this garden / to forget, to find a new beauty / in some terrible / wind-tortured place" ("Sheltered Garden").

Ten years earlier another poet dared to propose that Eurydice actually preferred her death to following Orpheus into the upper world. Preferred no longer belonging to him. Preferred no longer being seen as that mild, blue-eyed woman. Preferred a world (even an underworld) where her fate would now be hers alone: "She was deep within herself, like a woman heavy / with child. . . . / Like a fruit /

suffused with its own mystery and sweetness, / she was filled with her vast death. . . . / She had come into a new virginity / and was untouchable" ("Orpheus. Eurydice. Hermes"). And now, instead of *farewell,* the one word Eurydice utters when Hermes bends to tell her that Orpheus has turned around—the one word she utters is "*Who?*"

In still another, later poem by H. D., a poem entitled "Eurydice," the story becomes Eurydice's own, and it's Orpheus who serves as a constituent of that fate which *she* must suffer. As anguish gives way to anger, the silence that previously surrounded her is broken once and for all:

> For all your arrogance
> and your glance,
> I tell you this:
>
> such loss is no loss,
> such terror, such coils and strands and pitfalls
> of blackness,
> such terror
> is no loss;
>
> hell is no worse than your earth
> above the earth,
> hell is no worse.

(That H. D.'s poem was written, as her autobiographical writings suggest, in direct address to the failed Orphic figures in her life—to Richard Aldington, Ezra Pound, and D. H. Lawrence—adds a biting personal authority, and an equally biting cultural significance, to the fury of her assertions.)

It's as though, at this particular moment in the myth, the margin and the center change places. And in this sudden reversal—whose revisionist implications are as significant as any in the history of the myth—the very nature of poetry will undergo a sea change. The secrets Eurydice's voice release onto the complex tidal workings of this tale suffuse it with an urgency which the arts of our century have responded to with unprecedented zeal.

◆

Following Eurydice's second death, Orpheus is said to have tried again to cross the river around Hades. Having failed that, for seven days he sat on the banks and wept and fasted. For the next three years he lived without a woman, although, as Ovid tells us, "many women / Wanted this poet for their own, and many / Grieved over their rejection." Instead, "his love was given / To young boys only," and he began to explain to the Thracian men that this was really the wiser choice: "*enjoy that springtime, / Take those first flowers!*" [16]

There was one hill in particular, and on that hill a wide, green, shadeless plain where Orpheus would often go to sing. And when he sang, the shade from the surrounding woods drew near his crouching form. Oak trees, poplars, lindens, and beech, hazel, ash, and silver fir, sycamore, ilex, and willow tree—all would cluster to the hill and listen. One day, as he wedded his song to the music of his lyre, from a nearby hilltop a group of women caught sight of him. Excited from a night of celebrating their appointed Bacchic rites, these Maenads, we're told, rose up as one, and one of them, her hair streaming out in the morning air, cried out to the others around her, "Look there! / There is our despiser!" [17]

The first woman groaned and cast a spear at his singing mouth. Another hurled a heavy stone. Yet spear and stone, conquered by the power of the poet's song, fell harmlessly to the earth beside him. Still others gathered whatever weapons they could find, and before too long it seemed as though some furious warfare raged. (In a red-figured attic amphora, ca. 430 B.C., Orpheus is surrounded by a group of women—their hair bristling, their bodies covered in tattoos—bearing spears, arrows, farm implements, and stones.) Had it not been for the music of war, these weapons too would have fallen harmlessly to the ground; but the braying of trumpets, the pounding of drums, shrieks and howls, and the beating of breasts all rose to a pitch that drowned out the music of the poet's lyre. The well-aimed stones now reddened with blood. And then, as when barking dogs will come upon a wounded stag beside the game pits, the women viciously closed on him. The poet reached out imploringly—just as once he'd reached toward Eurydice—but for the first time ever in all his life, his wretched pleas touched no one.

◆

Equally varied in Orphic mythology are accounts of the *sparagmós*, of Orpheus's murder and dismemberment. Virgil has suggested that the Maenads were jealous of the poet's devotion to his dead wife's memory. Ovid tells us that the poet now shunned the attentions of women, perhaps in devotion to Eurydice, perhaps from a lack of interest in women, and gave his love to young boys only. Still earlier versions hypothesize that Orpheus had deliberately abandoned Eurydice in order to indulge his passion for boys. Reminiscent of Hera's blinding of Tiresias, less popular accounts have Orpheus struck by Zeus's thunderbolt for revealing sacred secrets. Whatever the case, it seems Orpheus no longer *saw* those Thracian women, no longer turned on them that gaze—that gaze which possessed the power to confer the shimmer of sexual identity. And having once been reduced to a sexual identity, how else could they respond, once that identity was removed, except with a murderous rage? Ultimately, the power of his gaze was most apparent, not when it consigned or even stigmatized a sexual identity, but when, by its withdrawal, it reduced to insignificance (or worse, invisibility) the identity it formerly bestowed.

In the aftermath of the Maenads' fury, Orpheus's limbs lay scattered about the bloody field. Birds, beasts, rocks, and river: all things grieved. The surrounding trees shook down their leaves like women tearing out their hair. And the wind in the trees made an anguished sound, like the souls of the dead released through the mournful voices of the living.

The sound of the wind as it moved through the trees? Eurydice, remember, was a dryad, an oak-tree nymph, and before her death trees would actually uproot themselves to listen to the music from

Orpheus's lyre. After her death, trees would come to the shadeless plain to provide some shelter for the poet's loss. And after Orpheus himself was killed, it was trees again that bent to mourn, like women pulling out their hair. In a ruthless reminder of her presence there, Eurydice's nature would figure forth in the punishment of the Maenads, for Bacchus now bound them all in rope, twisted their feet into gnarly roots, and planted them deep in the forest floor. In time, gripped by the unrelenting earth, the women watched in horror as, minute by minute, from the dark soil up, their bodies were covered over in bark: "Their breasts / Were oak, and oak their shoulders, and their arms / You well might call long branches and be truthful." [18]

◆

The river Hebrus, its waters overflowing with tears, lifted the poet's head and lyre and bore them out on its current—an ethereally beautiful image taken up repeatedly in nineteenth- and twentieth-century art to express both the pain and transcendence of the creative act. Miraculously, as these fragile vessels floated down the river, the lyre gave off a plangent sound, and the head responded by repeating the name *Eurydice*. In the end, they came to rest on the shores of the island of Lesbos, and Ovid describes how a serpent struck the dripping head. The lyre was taken by Jupiter and placed among the stars, and the head was buried in a prophetic shrine where it continues to serve as an oracle. Thereafter, both heaven and earth would have their voice, the Orphic song was released back into the universe, and the poet's art would live beyond the terrible brutality that marked his end.

So that his son should be entombed at the foot of Mount Olympos, Apollo sent the Muses to gather the parts of his dismembered body. (It is said that even now the nightingales near that tomb, suffused with the memory of Orpheus's song, still sing more beautifully than anywhere else in the world.) Meanwhile, the soul of Orpheus had slipped off silently into the earth. And there he journeyed, searching those places he'd known before, searching at length the fields of the blesséd, until he came at last to Eurydice and took her in his arms.

We're told their shades still wander there, like Heathcliff and Cathy ghosting the moors, side by side, or Orpheus following, or Eurydice trailing behind: a tableau of human love and loss, the end of a spiritual journey which remains, to this day, the unfinished story of poetry and poets.

Writing the Poet,
Unwriting the Poem

Notes Toward
an *Ars Poetica*

I've been asked to select a poem of my own, a poem which either by accident or design might reasonably serve as an *ars poetica.* Requests like that, flattering as they are, can quickly give rise (in my case anyway) to a disabling self-consciousness or, worse, to the murky satisfactions of the flimflam man. For if the process of making a poem is, as I've come to believe, generative and instinctual, then at some level and to some degree the process of speaking for one's own poems inevitably becomes degenerative and methodical, a kind of unwriting of what's been written. And at the end of the day it is hard not to feel that poems all secretly aspire to persist in a state beyond the reach of words—especially those of their author.

Because of that, I'm reluctant to impose my own deliberations on the poem's more covert tendencies, to try to make explicit those features which the poem has chosen instead to insinuate, override, or transmute. Which is to say, I won't attempt anything approaching an explication. But not to shrink from the request altogether, I've decided to alter the assignment a little.

I've decided to use the poem as occasion to touch upon certain oddities which, over the years, writing poems has schooled me to think are the unique properties of poetry. Lumped together these oddities have led to the opinion that, more often than not, the act of writing is better served by allowing the poem to speak for itself, as free as possible from my own interventions, and even (or especially) when *what* the poem wants to say mulishly opposes what I'd actually like it to say.

In light of that disclosure, I'll attempt to describe the means by which the poem I've chosen constitutes its own way of making, how it breaks the ground for its own momentary *ars poetica*—or the *ars poetica* of its moment—and how, through the constituents of its language, it establishes its own priorities.

Abandoned Railway Station

The agent's office like an abbey chancel.
The smell of wood smoke from the baggage stalls.
Large empty walls, and a water-stain,
ultramarine, like a fresco of Perseus,
head in hand, fleeing the golden falchion.

The silence of thousands of last good-byes.
A dried ink pad. Stanchioned ceiling.
And a cognate, terra-cotta dust over
everything, with the on-tiptoe atmosphere
of a *boule de neige* before it's shaken.

I've chosen this particular poem because it's one in which nothing really happens, about a place in which whatever happened before now looms in shadowy afterlife, in a past welling up through the thin-spun gauze of the present. This is significant to me because I've come to feel that, like Eliot's rose garden in "Little Gidding," poetry flourishes at "the intersection of the timeless moment," a moment Eliot describes, not as an absence, but as a confluence of all the rivers of time: "Never and always."[1] And here was a place, an abandoned train station, a ramshackle junction of time and space, which invited me (or should I say it invited the poem?) to contemplate both the literal and metaphorical meaning of such things.

One of the principal attractions of an abandoned place—especially a place that has formerly served as a threshold between two other worlds—is not so much the presentness of its location (its residual powers of representation) as the heady atmosphere of its dislocations (its accruing powers of enchantment). This is the same difference one experiences, say, between the Civil War museum in Gettysburg and the open battlefield beyond its doors. For an abandoned place, the insistence on the presence of *what's-not-here*—those post-sentiments and hauntings—is what defines the character of *what-is-here*.

This sensation travels back in time and forward in psychological space, for while an abandoned place retains the imprint of its earlier life (the wood smoke, water stains, last good-byes), it also projects us forward into a reverie on those myriad moments of departure and arrival by which we come to define our lives. As Eliot went on to say, "Every phrase and every sentence is an end and a beginning."

In many ways these Proustian relations correspond to a similar set of relations we've established between reality, memory, and dream— or, if you will, between art, the past, and the imagination. As Nabokov once commented in a lecture on Proust, "The key to the problem of reestablishing the past turns out to be the key to art." Through the impersonal dark of Mnemosyne's gaze pass the mysteries of our most personal glimmerings; and as my poem soon discovered, that bittersweet experience of the crossroads is replicated somehow in the "on-tiptoe atmosphere" which precedes the shaking of a *boule de neige*.

It may be that the central fascination of any poem (or of any lyric poem, at least) is contained in a similar suspension. Like the tension-surface of an over-filled glass, the village scene is pitched at the brink of being, a being that comes in a dreamlike spill—for what does the snowfall signify except the poignant rhythms of the dreaming mind? This is followed, of course, by an opposite and equally powerful feeling, and before too long that swirling mesmeric moment gives way, the lobed flecks turn precipitate, and flake by flake consciousness settles back into place: the village scene is banked in snow.

We live between two darknesses—the prenatal and the post-mortem—and we hurtle inexorably from the one to the other at a speed, as Nabokov noted, of some forty-five hundred heartbeats an hour. The experience of our daily lives is largely concerned with marking that passage in linear ways, by proximity to the fact of our birth, on the one hand, and by the anticipation of our death, on the other. In a very different way, the experience of poetry is the experience of recapitulation, a kind of trans-temporal immersion, a baptism in the liquid element of time: the past in the process of becoming the present, the present in the process of becoming the future. Looking back, I suspect that sensation had something to do with my attraction to poetry in the first place. What I loved then, what I love now, is that heart-stopping sense of *bilocation*, that body rush of simultaneity (both spatial and temporal) which a poem's slow fall of images fixes in a reader's mind.

And since whatever we love informs the spirit of whatever we make, I suspect writing poems provides me with a way of denying, or of keeping at bay, the privileged status of the present—and of keeping at hand some quickening sense of the contemporaneity of the past. Poetry reminds me, to return to "Little Gidding," that "the end of all our exploring / Will be to arrive where we started / And know the place for the first time." It is a Homeric knowledge, and its drama inheres in its powers of negative capability, in its capacity to hold within its grasp that ebb and tide of memory. It's as if, while gazing through the snowfall of a *boule de neige*—and no matter how remote the scene beyond—one gazes in the direction of one's own life.

Shelley in Ruins

~~~~~

"Ozymandias" Undone

However quaint it might seem to current trends in literary discourse, I'm unwilling to abandon the idea that it's from poems themselves that we learn the most about poetry—from that intimate and strangely alchemical process by which a poem imparts both the sense and sensibility of its author. And in keeping with that idea, I'd like to take a single poem and attempt to figure out what, if anything, it has to say about its own inner workings. That is, I'd like to let the poem speak both for and about itself, its author, and its reader.

This is how Wallace Stevens, in "Peter Quince at the Clavier," marks out that three-part structure of relations:

> Just as my fingers on these keys
> Make music, so the selfsame sounds
> On my spirit make a music, too.
>
> Music is feeling, then, not sound;
> And thus it is that what I feel,
> Here in this room, desiring you,
>
> Thinking of your blue-shadowed silk,
> Is music. It is like the strain
> Waked in the elders by Susanna.

As these carefully modulated shadings detail, we move from the work (the "fingers on these keys"), to the issue of that work (the "music"), to the effect of that issue (a "feeling"). And it doesn't end there. For the poem's profounder intuition is that the resulting inner vibration—that impression made by the music made by those fingers on the keys—is not a sound at all, but a feeling. Hence simple human physical desire ("what I feel, / Here in this room, desiring you") must also be a form of music. And just as the emotions are the means by which we know and ultimately apprehend the arts, so too the arts are the means by which we know and ultimately apprehend the emotions.

To complete this movement, Stevens comes full circle by reconnecting our passions (the "music" of our feelings) to the worlds of art and experience: "It is like the strain / Waked in the elders by Susanna." With uncanny precision, Stevens distills this moment into a single signifying noun—"strain"—which denotes both the raw physical exertion of the passions and a passage of musical expression.

All of which brings me to ask, if that's how a poem makes itself known, then how do we manage to know a poem in all its manifold meanings? Not only how do we read a poem, but how does a poem come to its reading? One speculative answer, modestly tendered: the process of coming to a poem's meaning is, at some level, as *post facto* for the poet as it is for the reader. The meaning of a poem, like the "meaning" of a dream, may conceal itself from the poet or reveal itself only in slow and indeterminate ways. Moreover, what (and how much) a poem discloses to its author is limited precisely to what (and how much) it discloses to its readers—because *that is all there is to know,* those "selfsame sounds" that on our "spirit make a music."

For those reasons, a poem's "grand elementary principle of pleasure," as Wordsworth called it, only deepens in time, only grows more meaningful as it takes on the resonance of all its myriad readers, readings, and misreadings. As the distinguished Renaissance scholar A. Richard Turner has observed, our love and understanding of Leonardo's paintings would be profoundly diminished without the manifold chorus of (often contradictory) readings which people like Vasari, Sir Joshua Reynolds, Goethe, Walter Pater, Valéry, and Freud have brought to them.

Oscar Wilde, reflecting on Pater's essay on the *Mona Lisa,* put the

argument even more forcefully: "Who, again, cares whether Mr. Pater has put into the portrait of Mona Lisa something that Leonardo
never dreamed of? The painter may have been merely the slave of an
archaic smile. . . . But when I pass into the cool galleries of the Palace
of the Louvre . . . I murmur to myself, 'She is older than the rocks
among which she sits; like the vampire, she has been dead many times,
and learned the secrets of the grave; and has been a diver in deep seas,
and keeps their fallen day about her.'" [1] For Wilde, Leonardo's painting has become more meaning-full than it was before Pater's essay;
more significantly, Leonardo's painting has revealed to Pater a secret
about which Leonardo—though he created the secret—apparently
knew nothing.

Since interpretive access to a work of art is gained, according to
Stevens, through "feeling"—through that inner vibration, that impression made by the "music" made by those "fingers on these keys"
—then a work of art inevitably contains more "strains" of meaning
than either its creator or its viewer could possess in full. Although the
poem is the poet's creation—just as the dream is the dreamer's creation—it is also the repository for secrets of which the poet has no
conscious knowledge. With that in mind, I want to hold up to Percy
Bysshe Shelley's seductively enigmatic sonnet, "Ozymandias," this
mirroring premise: the poem writes the poet.

✦

Even though there is, as we'll see, a certain transgressive element to
my choice, I've selected "Ozymandias" more by impulse than design.
Furthermore, this happens to be a poem about which much has already been written, and so, one might ask, what more is there to say?
Obviously, history forces particular issues to the forefront of any
conversation, and the issue here may be located within that phrase so
often thrown around these days: "artistic integrity."

We might begin by wrenching that phrase from its normally high-
handed usage, or at least we might bend it to mean, not the haughty
inviolability of the aesthetic experience, but the integral power of a
work of art to insist on certain meanings—unpleasant and even un-

wanted meanings, meanings that may run counter to meanings intended by its creator. Artistic integrity may be seen, then, not as a shield for the artist against a censorious public, but as a shield for the work against a censorious artist.

This is Shelley's poem, presented in its entirety:

I met a traveller from an antique land,
Who said—"Two vast and trunkless legs of stone
Stand in the desert . . . Near them, on the sand,
Half sunk a shattered visage lies, whose frown,
And wrinkled lip, and sneer of cold command,
Tell that its sculptor well those passions read
Which yet survive, stamped on these lifeless things,
The hand that mocked them, and the heart that fed;
And on the pedestal, these words appear:
My name is Ozymandias, King of Kings,
Look on my Works, ye Mighty, and despair!
Nothing beside remains. Round the decay
Of that colossal Wreck, boundless and bare
The lone and level sands stretch far away."

Somewhat surprisingly, since this sonnet comes to us from a historical and cultural moment so different from our own, those fourteen lines (with the possible exception of the one word "visage") are free of archaisms and antiquated phrasings. On the whole, they seem disarmingly straightforward and unembellished, especially so when we stop to recall that they're written by a poet who once referred to his beloved as "Sweet Benediction in the eternal Curse! / Veiled Glory of this lampless Universe! / Thou Moon beyond the clouds! Thou living Form / Among the Dead! Thou Star above the Storm!" ("Epipsychidion"). To enlist Stevens's terminology, the "music," the "feeling" of "Ozymandias"—austere, inexorable, disembodied, as if blown by dry winds across the "lone and level sands" of its closing line—is played in a very different key.

But what does that observation tell us? And how has time accounted for that difference? A brief survey of its literary history reveals that popular opinion periodically undergoes a sea change. Newman Ivey White's definitive, two-volume, fourteen hundred–page biography (1940) never once mentions "Ozymandias," though it was included in Palgrave's *Golden Treasury* (1861), and today is widely considered one of Shelley's finest lyric achievements—the only one of his sonnets, according to another Shelley scholar, Desmond King-Hele (1960), that "can bear comparison with Shakespeare's."

The reason for this ambivalence is both more and less baffling than might first appear, for the rise and fall of the poem's reputation is inversely correspondent to the rise and fall of the overall reputation of Shelley's work. Those who are drawn to this poem appear to admire it, not because it's quintessential Shelley, but because it's so out of keeping with the Shelley style; likewise, those who dislike or ignore it appear to do so for the very same reason. Where Shelley is normally oracular, extravagant, intuitional, and transportive, here he is detached, ironic, skeptical, and cool—as though his Orphean lute had been traded in for the slide-rule of the Metaphysical poet.

❧

Perhaps now we should ask a more substantive question: So who was Ozymandias, and how did he end up in Shelley's poem? At one level we know that this was the Greek name for Ramses II, and that inscribed on an Egyptian temple, as recorded by Diodorus Siculus, is the high-and-mighty sentence, "I am Ozymandias, king of kings; if anyone wishes to know what I am and where I lie, let him surpass me in some of my exploits." We know that in the autumn of 1817, around the time of the poem's composition, Egyptian subjects were making quite a stir in England, and that the British Museum had just taken in a collection of pieces from the Empire of the Ramses—pieces including the Rosetta Stone and a large-scale figure of Ramses II. We also know that, following a visit to the museum with Horace Smith, Shelley proposed that they each compose a sonnet on the subject.

Still, that evidence is largely circumstantial, and, as such, it leads us back to the beginning. But what if we were to ask a knottier question? What if we were to break taboo and ask ourselves: Who was

Shelley anyway, and how does *he* figure in the poem called "Ozymandias"? The son of a member of Parliament, Shelley was a poet who in his youth—and since he died at twenty-nine, I use that term in a relative sense—passionately believed in the role of the poet as world-reformer, political activist, the agent of justice, and the enemy of commerce, royalty, and religion. This was the poet who, at eighteen, sent copies of his pamphlet *The Necessity of Atheism* to all the faculty and administrators at Oxford (where he was a student at the time) and to all the bishops in the United Kingdom—a quixotic gesture for which he was promptly and unceremoniously expelled.

This was the same poet who, months later, living in Dublin, attempted to organize the Irish into "the society of peace and love"; and who, having failed at that, resettled in Wales where he sent out into the waiting world yet another hopeful pamphlet, *A Declaration of Rights*, which he launched into the air in bright balloons, and onto the sea in toy boats and corked bottles. By then he was nineteen and midway through his first significant poem, *Queen Mab*, a long verse narrative studded with lectures on politics, religion, and society. In an 1812 letter to the philosopher William Godwin, he described that period of his life this way: "I could not descend to common life: the sublime interest of poetry, lofty and exalted achievements, the proselytism of the world, the equalization of its inhabitants, were to me the soul of my soul."

"Ozymandias" benefits, I think, from being read in light of that boundless moral fervor, in light of that age-old, back-and-forth struggle—as germane today as it was back then—between the social and aesthetic demands of an art. Although Shelley was only twenty-five at the time of its composition, his earlier utopian claims on the world, and his role as crusader within that world, had been seriously tested by events in his life: the abandonment of his children and his wife, Harriet Westbrook, to elope with Mary Godwin; the suicide of Mary's half-sister, for which Shelley felt partially responsible; the death and possible suicide of Harriet; the scandal surrounding Mary's step-sister, Claire Clairmont, pregnant by Byron though assumed by many to be pregnant by Shelley; the court's denial of custody of his children by Harriet; and Shelley fearful that he'd soon lose custody of his children by Mary as well. . . . The list goes on and on.

His own small "society of peace and love" had proven to be anything but; his political aspirations had likewise come to naught; and his poetry was greeted with widespread public indifference. It's as though the magnitude of his disillusionment—matched only by the magnitude of his early ambitions—would suffuse this poem with a sobering, retrospective self-contempt. Though it upholds Shelley's lifelong disdain for despots and kings, and though the poem is normally read as a political tract to express that disdain, it's also tempting to see it as a moment when Shelley steps back to observe *himself*. When, through the eyes of posterity, he steps back to observe that failed persona—that venerated, long-suffering, supersensitive "*Me*," as he described it in *Julian and Maddalo*—"who am as a nerve o'er which do creep / The else unfelt oppressions of this earth."

◆

It is tempting, in fact, to see "Ozymandias" as an instance of the poem revising the poet—as an instance of the poet caught in that painfully clarifying light which poetry and dreams can cast on us. As Emily Dickinson advised, "Tell all the Truth but tell it slant," an injunction intended not, as is often assumed, to make poetry more difficult for its own sake, but to make it more true for the poet's. Since there are certain truths ("Too bright for our infirm Delight") that can't be faced directly ("Or every man be blind"), one of poetry's important functions is to keep alive, by telling it "slant," those truths from which we'd otherwise hide. By telling it slant, poetry, like dream, both keeps and discloses its secrets.

If there's any basis for this (admittedly) odd idea, then it may be that there's more of Shelley in that "shattered visage" than we first perceive. For are the grand delusions of a tyrant who boasted "Look on my Works, ye Mighty, and despair!" all that different from those of a poet who'd once aspired to "lofty and exalted achievements, the proselytism of the world, the equalization of its inhabitants"? Perhaps pressing into being through the features of that disintegrated stone is a self with whom Shelley once felt a strong affinity—a self he now looked back to find betrayed by destiny, abandoned of hope, and lying in the rubble of its own exuberant idealism.

Strangely enough—and herein lies the poem's unspoken promise to the poet—within that bitter self-negation resides an affirmation. For out of "the decay / Of that colossal Wreck," the world-reformer will discover, at last, a more truly self-centering relationship to his art. As true for Shelley as it was for Keats, the death of the self was prerequisite to the birth of the poet. And by the time he'd write his *Defence of Poetry*—composed a year before his death, four years after "Ozymandias"—Shelley would reverse himself to claim that a poet "would do ill to embody his own conceptions of right and wrong, which are usually those of his place and time, in his poetical creations, which participate in neither."

That's quite a turnabout. And no doubt it will sound to us as suspiciously absolute, and as politically dubious, as his earlier claim to William Godwin. But what's interesting here is not simply, or not only, what he's saying, but the process by which he came to say it.

◆

That eerie sense of detachment which distinguishes "Ozymandias" from others in the Shelley canon comes about through a complex layering of voices and an equally complex layering of times: a story within a story within a story. We have, first off, what might be called the poem's "frame," a tale recounted by an anonymous "I"—a narrator one might naturally associate with the poet.

And *his* story holds a second story, as told by a "traveler from an antique land," a story behind which the original narrator quickly disappears. In some far away and some long ago place, so the traveler is reported to say, there exists a desert in which he'd found "Two vast and trunkless legs of stone" and, nearby, "a shattered visage." And that was all, "Nothing beside remains." No trace of those achievements of which an inscription on the pedestal grandly boasts, "Look on my Works, ye Mighty, and despair!"

But the time the traveler refers us to refers us back to another time, to yet another story within *his* story. A time preceding the pedestal and the trunkless legs. A time from which a message was launched, as in a toy boat or corked bottle, onto a sea of random connections which have borne it here today. That message appears to have something to do with "those passions . . . / Which yet survive," though the artist who "mocked them" ("mocked" here means *copied*, not *ridiculed*), and the king whose heart they roused, are now reduced to "lifeless things." The message appears to exist somewhere in the juxtaposition of what survives to what is swallowed up in the inexorable movement of time.

A curious thing has happened. For the role of the artist, while linked by those passions to the role of the sovereign, is also implicitly distinguished from it. What survives of the ruler—or, in my reading, the youthful idealist Shelley—is not, as the inscription claims, "my Works" but a subordinate and reducible disposition, that "sneer of cold command." What survives of the artist, while reducible to neither the work nor the disposition, still, of necessity, contains them both (the "sneer" is inseparable from the stone on which it's carved).

More significantly, the artist's making has somehow managed to outstrip time. For this reason we might safely assume that the poem is less concerned with Ozymandias as an emblem of those tyrants Shelley deplored—after all, whether tyrant or benevolent leader, the fate of Ozymandias would remain the same—and more concerned with that carefully nuanced chain of connections which has accurately "read," skillfully "mocked," and successfully preserved "those passions."

Of course, that process only begins with the sculptor. Had it ended with him, his works, like Shakespeare's "gilded monuments / Of princes," would have long been lost to "sluttish time." For in order to keep those passions alive, there is a second artist (whose art is telling) who has had to read and record their movement: that mysterious "traveler from an antique land," without whose story we'd know nothing of this movement. And then, as well, as we circle back through the layers of the poem, we're reminded of a crucial, tertiary link: the poet himself, the poet who composed the poem "Ozymandias," the poem which contains and keeps alive both the traveler's story and the sculptor's stone.

Oddly enough, the poet (or the poem's speaker in any case) proves the least present figure in the poem. He ostensibly speaks only the first ten words of the sonnet, and those are directed elsewhere: "I met a traveller from an antique land / Who said. . . ." So where is he, this poet who, after a visit to the British Museum, proposed to a friend that they each attempt a sonnet on the subject? The poet who, through a mysterious confluence of events in his life, sat down to write a poem unlike any he'd written before?

It's appealing to imagine that, for the moment anyway, there was no poet. That the poem was composed in that stillness which lies between the death of one self and the birth of another, or that the poet who *would be* had not yet come into being, while the poet who *was* was rubble. It's appealing to imagine that, at most, there existed a consciousness, the faintest whisper of a consciousness, gazing back over the prospect of its own past life. And what did this consciousness see? To borrow words spoken about another famously deconstructed statue—the great stone statue of General Du Puy in *Notes Toward a Supreme Fiction:* "There never had been, never could be, such / A man."

♦

"Ozymandias" may serve as a cautionary tale—conveyed to the poet midway in his writing life—about the futility of worldly ambition and the transience of fame. Yet it's a poem with a darker interior as well, for at the heart of its revelation lies nothing less than a harrowing encounter with the desolate experience of self-extinction: "Round the decay / Of that colossal Wreck, boundless and bare / The lone and level sands stretch far away." The shock of that experience may account for the almost posthumous tone that attends its lines. And the effect of those lines remains, for me, one of the more urgent, unsettling, and unmediated moments in Shelley's work.

Whatever the relation of the details of the poem to the details of Shelley's life, the mere fact of its freakishness, its subversiveness in the Shelley canon, makes it a telling text to ponder. Telling because it points up the power, too rarely acknowledged, too rarely conceded, of the poem's instinct to override the poet's self-determinations—be they political, aesthetic, religious, honorific, romantic, or otherwise. It may be that poetry remains the only language we possess to tell ourselves the most unspeakable truths about ourselves; and it may be that the poem is the language, to alter Oscar Wilde's meaning, "of what we pray for, or perhaps of what, having prayed for, we fear that we may receive."

Eating the Angel,
Conceiving the Sun

How Does Poetry Think?

In the last lectures Heidegger gave before retiring from the university in 1952—the first he'd been permitted to give since the end of the Second World War—he embarked on a series of meditations on the endlessly riddling subject of thinking.[1] During the course of those lectures he would form the opinion that science doesn't think, that pure thinking lies closer in fact to the ground of poetry, and that the only thing worth thinking about is what is truly unthinkable.

One can't say for sure to what extent, or with what inflection, he might have intended that secondary sense which "unthinkable" carries in English, that sense of the dark, the repressed, the forbidden; or to what extent his opinions were shadowed by the fact that, ten years earlier, he'd been banned from teaching for having served in the Nazi people's militia. But for the moment anyway we'll allow those meanings to play alongside the more ordinary one: that which is simply inconceivable. And if indeed it's true that thinking lies closer to poetry than science—by "an abyss of essence," as the lectures conclude—then perhaps there's something to be learned about thinking by asking some questions about poetry. Perhaps, as well, there's something to be learned about poetry's art by inquiring into the famously extrasensory manner by which it's known to think.

Since some form of thinking inevitably precedes the physical act of writing out a line of poetry, however automatic or spontaneous it seems, our questions should probably begin with that period before the words are scratched to life. That is, what do you know beforehand when you sit down to write a poem? At what level is it consciously determined what that poem will think about? And when, in advance, you already have a "subject" in mind, what does it mean, as so often happens, when the poem insists, through the countervailing logic of its images and sounds, on diverting the poem in another direction altogether?

In the early drafts of *The Waste Land,* for instance, one encounters a poem evolving, not toward the establishment and articulation of its original meaning, but toward that meaning's sublimation and conversion. One small but revealing example derives from an anecdote told by Ezra Pound. When he questioned Eliot's use of an epigraph from Conrad's *Heart of Darkness* (a passage that ended "He cried in a whisper at some image, at some vision,—he cried out twice, a cry that was no more than a breath—'The horror! the horror!'"), Eliot responded defensively, "It is much the most appropriate I can find, and somewhat elucidative." But as Eliot would soon acknowledge, appropriateness and elucidation form a governance the poem will soon subvert.

Accordingly, the Conrad epigraph was eventually replaced by the now-famous passage, in Latin and Greek, from Petronius: "For once I saw with my very own eyes the Sibyl of Cumae hanging in a cage, and when the boys said to her, 'Sibyl, what do you want?' she answered, 'I want to die.'" The instructive forthrightness of the first epigraph gives way to an elusive intertextuality in the second; in the first the meaning comes to the reader; in the second the reader must come to the meaning.

Still, a poem's self-governing instincts remain largely overlooked by literary criticism; indeed, the bulk of recent commentary on poetry, marked by fixed ideological purposes, appears to proceed from an opposite assumption, and supports the impression that poetry, like criticism, is bounded by forethought and caution. But poems will often prove least responsive when we've decided in advance what we want them to say. And is it merely quixotic when poets claim (as they often do) that they're most engaged, most "called into being" (in Heidegger's phrase), at those very moments when they're only discovering as they write what they're actually writing about? And even then, even in those most fortuitous times, aren't they actually discovering a meaning it's safe to say they weren't in possession of moments before?

An affirmative response to those questions would, presumably, locate meaning somewhere beyond the poet's reach, an idea fraught with murky implications for the already mysterious process of writing. And in apparent contradiction to that age-old advice handed out like gospel in our writing schools—"Write about what you know the best"—it would seem to suggest a reasonable alternative: "Write about what you know the least, about that which you find the most unthinkable." As Heidegger explained it in a passage inspired by Rilke, only then are we caught in the draft of thinking, for "what withdraws from us, draws us along by its very withdrawal." And, "whenever man is properly drawing that way, he is thinking—even though he may still be far away from what withdraws, even though the withdrawal may remain as veiled as ever." [2]

Like Aeneas, the poet sets sail for an ever-receding shore, and to follow that voyage we'll shift our focus from the *thought about* to the *thinking* itself. Or, to pose it in the form of a paradox, we'll shift our focus to a kind of thinking which thinks about what cannot be thought. The issue appears to hinge on what, exactly, declares itself as "thought-provoking," and here Heidegger devises a plain distinction: "Some things are food for thought in themselves, intrinsically, so to speak, innately. And some things make an appeal to us to give them thought, to turn toward them in thought: to think them." [3]

This is a sophisticated distinction disguised in the street clothes of figurative language, and, as such, it leaves one wondering about the practical forms it takes. That is, how is it manifest in the speech acts of any particular poem? Perhaps we can begin to pursue an answer by calling to mind, however briefly, two of the more celebrated examples of "thinking" poems this century has produced, Rainer Maria Rilke's *Duino Elegies* and Wallace Stevens's *Notes Toward a Supreme Fiction.*

◆

With a mournfully, almost liturgically chastened sweep of the hand—part Shakespearean, part young Werther—Rilke's great epic of yearning begins:

> Who, if I cried, would hear me among the angelic
> orders? And even if one of them suddenly
> pressed me against his heart, I should fade
> in the strength of his stronger existence.

And so, in those much-quoted opening lines, lines we're told arrived unbidden as the poet paced the windy bastions of Schloss Duino in the winter of 1911, Rilke introduces a figure of thought, an angel, a figure he quickly comes to see he'll never be able to think:

> For Beauty's nothing
> but the beginning of Terror we're still just able to bear,
> and why we adore it so is because it serenely
> disdains to destroy us. Each single angel is terrible.
> And so I keep down my heart, and swallow the call-note
> of depth-dark sobbing.

Rilke's fearsome angels serve, it appears, as an example of that which Heidegger claimed was innately "food for thought," for their aerial presence becomes, in time, the obverse of, and the nourishment for, our deepest spiritual hungers. In the grand Platonic sense, his angels represent an out-reaching form of education (from *educere: e* 'out' + *ducere* 'to lead'). And in the early Christian mystical sense, they also correspond to what Paul declared was the herald of a new humanity, "the unsearchable riches" of Christ. Rather than turning us inward—that neo-Romantic notion of the solitary, solipsistic life—Rilke's angels gradually lead us out of ourselves. What in them gives us to think is precisely what is lacking in us; what in them gives us to think is therefore wholly unthinkable.

In both nature and action, Rilke observed, angels surpass us to the very same degree that God surpasses them. And then, in a letter to his Polish translator: "The angel of the Elegies is that creature in whom the transformation of the visible into the invisible, which we are accomplishing, appears already consummated. . . . The angel of the elegies is that being who vouches for the recognition in the invisible of a higher order of reality.—Hence 'terrible' to us, because we, its lovers and transformers, do still cling to the visible."[4] But if angels bear the measure of our own inadequacy, they also affirm the quiet dignity of all our noblest yearnings. Because of that, their distance from us functions as both a promise and a reproach, and it's through that nagging paradox that they provided Rilke "food for thought," and in surprisingly literal ways. If we ever hope to attain them—and in Rilke it's their exemplary nature that is "terrible" and attractive—we must take them into ourselves, we must feed off their examples, we must, so to speak, eat angel.

In other words, if we can't enter them through our thoughts, then perhaps they can enter us (in an oddly conceived transubstantiation) through the vehicle of our bodies: "This world, seen no longer with the eyes of men . . . is perhaps my real task."[5] This isn't exactly anthropophagy, cannibalism, the consuming of one of our species, but it is a kind of theophagy (*Take, eat, this is my body*), a consuming of god or the divine, the incorporation of a life force which transcends our own. And like all truly religious spirits, Rilke sees his charge as divinely absolute: "You must change your life" ("Archaic Torso of Apollo"). Which meant no less than setting his thoughts on a "higher order of reality." Which meant no less than standing in the draught of a thinking toward something that can't be thought.

One sign of how agonizing that labor was: Following those first clairvoyant lines, it would take another decade before Rilke would finish the *Elegies*. And even then they would come to him fitfully, almost against his flagging will, in two brief but electrifying blocks of time—periods of "monstrous obedience," as he later described them—in 1912 and 1922. Rilke once said of Tolstoy that he "made a

dragon out of life so as to be the hero who fought it." And it might
be said of Rilke that he made an angel out of human imperfection so
as to be, like Jacob, the mortal destined to wrestle with it.

♦

If those "deadly birds of the soul" provided Rilke "food for thought,"
then it might be argued that, for Wallace Stevens, Reality belonged to
that second category Heidegger describes, of things that "appeal to us
to give them thought." And what in Reality appeals to Stevens is the
very fact that it's *outside thought*, that, in his word, it's "inconceivable":
"Not to be realized because not to / Be seen, not to be loved nor hated
because / Not to be realized" ("It Must Be Abstract," canto VI).

That explains the nature of Reality's remoteness, its inaccessibility to us and our language; and yet, as the very first canto reminds us,
there it stands, "The inconceivable idea of the sun." And as it stands,
"Washed in the remotest cleanliness of a heaven / That has expelled
us and our images," it appeals to us to give it thought, to turn toward
it in thought, to think it—though *it*, paradoxically, is that which
finally "Must bear no name . . . but be / In the difficulty of what
it is to be" (canto I). The unthinkable in Stevens is not (or not simply) a place which meaning finds hard to grasp but a place before
which meaning is, like the water bead on a white-hot pan, instantly
extinguished.

Unlike Rilke's angels, Stevens's Reality never becomes "food for
thought" for the simple reason that nothing in it is consumable (in
the way, for example, that an angel's death-consciousness is), nothing
in it is exemplary. It exists beyond the moral order, and only through
the distortions of our own sadly projected egos do we turn it to such
purposes. On the other hand, Reality remains something toward
which our thoughts are drawn, drawn in spite of the crippling fact that
"poisonous // Are the ravishments of truth," those very thoughts we
think it with, "fatal to / The truth itself" (canto II).

Applying Heidegger's terminology, we might say that Stevens's
poem isn't "about" Reality at all—for language falls short of captur-
ing Reality by the very degree that it's brought to bear—it's about

Reality's withdrawal, about our own strangely implacable desire "to have what is not," to think what is finally unthinkable. Here again, Heidegger writes:

> What must be thought about turns away from man. It withdraws from him. But how can we have the least knowledge of something that withdraws from the beginning, how can we even give it a name? [A name like Phoebus, Stevens reminds us, "a name for something that never could be named."] Whatever withdraws, refuses arrival. But—withdrawing is not nothing. Withdrawal is an event. In fact, what withdraws may even concern and claim man more essentially than anything present that strikes and touches him.[6]

As Stevens has observed, poetry plays out an ongoing engagement with "the inaccessibility of the abstract," though abstract here means, not opposed to concrete, but separate from, withdrawing.

◆

So, when we sit down to write, what do we intend to do, and how do we intend to do it? More importantly, how does one go about putting oneself "in the pull" of thinking? The question of our somehow choosing our subjects Heidegger puts to rest: "What is thought-provoking, what gives us to think, is then not anything that we determine, not anything that only we are instituting, only we are proposing."[7] Or, as he states it more crisply in his gnomic poem/essay "The Thinker as Poet," "We never come to thoughts. They come to us."[8]

And yet who among us, at one time or another, hasn't had the impression of choosing the thing we'd like our poem to say? At the same time, who among us hasn't had the impression, on just such occasions, of the poem starting to veer away, with a mind of its own, toward its own set of strict concerns?

In the year that Germany invaded Poland, W. H. Auden concluded his poem "September 1, 1939" with the premonitory line: "We must love one another or die." Fifteen years later he revised that line to read: "We must love one another and die." In the tragic arc between those versions one can chart the brutal disillusionment of an age; and one begins to understand how poetry undermines our conscious intentions. For within that single syllable "or" lay the basis for the liberal humanist hopes Auden harbored in those days; but within that subversive alternative "and" lay a darker intuition, a thought beyond the reach of thought, the unthinkable prospect that world events issue from a chaos in the human heart. Applying Heidegger's maxim, it may be said that Auden came to the first version of the poem, the second came to Auden. Of the first version he would later remark, "It is the most dishonest poem I have ever written."

And here is where I'd like to suggest, in yet another departure from common sense, that therein lies the crux of the matter, the one perhaps sure distinction, quantitative issues of verse aside, one can draw between poetry and prose: poetry's stubborn, inborn, implausible resolve to tell the truth, however incongruous, however insufferable the telling may be. Poetry is intent on saying those things we're most determined to hide, even from ourselves.

Two chance but not unrelated comments may shed some light on this subject. The first comes from a letter Elizabeth Bishop wrote to Robert Lowell about some difficulties she'd encountered with a piece of prose: "That desire to get things straight and tell the truth—it's impossible not to tell the truth in poetry, I think, but in prose it keeps eluding me in the funniest way."[9] The second comes from an interview with Richard Wilbur: "I know a lot of people, poets, who are not consciously religious, but find themselves forever compromised by their habit of asserting the relevance of all things to each other. And poetry being a kind of truth-telling (it's pretty hard to lie in poetry), I think that these people must be making, whether they like it or not, what are ultimately religious assertions."[10]

It's almost impossible to lie in poetry, both poets tell us parenthetically. But what are we to make of this? To pursue a roundabout analogy: In Freud's writings on hysteria, we learn that there are moments in childhood which inscribe themselves so indelibly on us that we're doomed to repeat, in ways that may remain a mystery to us, their inherent patterns and forms. This *repetition compulsion*, as Freud called it, was considered a governing drive in the unconscious—a drive which supplanted even the "pleasure principle" in the hierarchy of powers that determine unconscious behavior. The French philosopher Jean-François Lyotard even ventured to suggest that what we call "style" in writing is just such a case of hysterical repetition—an irrepressible urge to assert a pattern repeatedly.

This simplifies matters far too much, but while setting aside the question of illness (the mind's complexities are not, by nature, a "disorder," however inscrutable they appear), I'd like to suggest that a poet's relation to the poem is, in many ways, correspondent to the hysteric's relation to memory (Mnemosyne, remember, is the mother of the Muses). At least it's correspondent to the degree that the *process* of writing—over and against one's *intentions* in writing—makes "telling a lie" impossible, just as the willed deviation from a hysterical pattern is instantly erased, or overridden, once the will relents: "We must love one another or die" becomes "We must love one another and die." The conscious will stands corrected in time by the unconscious impulse to tell the truth.

This correspondence deepens when we consider that the poem's charge is to awaken memory to motion again, to recollect the remembranced body into the present tense, just as a childhood trauma is gathered by the body into the hysteric's living here and now. As Heidegger continues,

> Memory thinks back to something thought. But when it is the name of the Mother of the Muses, "Memory" does not mean just any thought of anything that can be thought. Memory is the gathering of thought upon what everywhere demands to be thought about first of all. . . . That is why poesy [poetry in the Greek sense of *poiesis*] is the water that at times flows backward toward the source, toward thinking as a thinking back, a recollection.[11]

This is the same distinction Freud draws between reminiscence, which he calls storytelling, and memory, which he calls remembering back to the origin of the story. It may be that Rilke considered a similar point when, in the first elegy, he referred to "the suspiration, / the uninterrupted news that grows out of silence." And Stevens may have thought along parallel lines when, in "Man and Bottle," he linked the violence of poetry, nature, and the human mind: "The poem lashes more fiercely than the wind, / As the mind, to find what will suffice, destroys / Romantic tenements of rose and ice."

But where does it come from, one might ask, all this "uninterrupted news"? Toward what does the direction backward lead? What lies behind that revisionist fury of poem and mind? And what do we gather in our moments of recollection? Pursued far enough, one answer to all those questions is, of course, the dead. As we know, for Stevens "Death is the mother of beauty" ("Sunday Morning"); for Rilke, it appears to be the mother of Being itself: "Only believe," he writes to Countess Margot Sizzo, "that it is a friend . . . our friend, just when we most passionately, most vehemently assent . . . to being here, to functioning, to Nature, to love. . . . Indeed, death (I adjure you to believe) is the true yea-sayer. It says only: Yes." [12]

To philosophize is to learn how to die, says Montaigne. And Hélène Cixous: "To begin (writing, living) we must have death." And: "The writer has a foreign origin; we do not know the particular nature of these foreigners, but we feel they feel there is an appeal, that someone is calling them back." [13] Rilke remains, first and foremost, a poet of the dead, and time after time in the *Elegies* the dead provide him access to his wildly "foreign origin." It may be that the root of that power derives from the soil of his largely unthinkable childhood, a childhood which appears to be no less daunting an object of thought than "those deadly birds of the soul." The following, from J. F. Hendry's *The Sacred Threshold: A Life of Rainer Maria Rilke*, provides a harrowing glimpse of that world:

René's hair was still long, as was a custom of the period, and he played with dolls. Even during the rare birthday parties, when he was allowed to entertain other children, or else play at "cooking" by him-self, his pursuits were inclined to be feminine. . . . Indeed until he was five, in accordance with [his mother's] grim pretence that he was not himself but a reincarnation of the daughter lost in infancy, René had to wear girl's clothes, and behave like a girl. He would stand outside the door and knock. When his mother called out, "Who is it?", he would squeak "Sophie." And when he entered, wearing a little house-frock with rolled-up sleeves, he was Mama's little Sophie, whose hair had to be plaited, so she should not be confused with the naughty boy. . . . Later she would ask him what had happened to "Sophie" and venture the opinion that "Sophie" must be dead. This Rilke would strenuously deny. . . .

If he could, René said, he would have been a girl for her sake. He enjoyed dressing up and standing before the mirror, until the day he became terrified because the girlish image was more real than he.[14]

Here was a child who carried within him the living presence of his dead sister; or perhaps more accurately, here was a child who carried within him his own secret, suppressed identity, while the liv-ing presence of his dead sister took over the features of his exter-nal life. In either case, the gulf between appearance and reality, es-sence and identity, surface and interior, proved enormous and, as one might guess, unthinkable in Rilke. In light of that, one can see the *Elegies* as an almost wholly involuntary effort to think that forbidden thought:

> Who shows a child as he really is? Who sets him
> in his constellation and puts the measuring-rod
> of distance in his hand? Who makes his death
> out of gray bread, which hardens — or leaves it there
> inside his round mouth, jagged as the core
> of a sweet apple? . . . Murderers are easy
> to understand. But this: that one can contain
> death, the whole of death, even before

life has begun, can hold it to one's heart
gently, and not refuse to go on living,
is *inexpressible.* (Elegy IV)

✦

So what do you know beforehand when you sit down to write a
poem? It may be that what you know, what's essential to know, is that
very thing you cannot know: the "inexpressible" in Rilke, the "unthinkable" in Heidegger, the "inconceivable" in Stevens. And who
hasn't been struck, while struggling to recall some fragment of the
past, by the sudden impression of sifting through ash; and then, by
the slowly dawning realization that who you are is composed of
what, perhaps only what, you can never reclaim from the rubble?

It may be that *that* is the thing which poets know, the presence
of that marked, presiding loss, the thought beyond the reach of
thought, the thought toward which our thoughts all turn when we're
in the draught of thinking. And given the willed uncertainties such
knowledge requires—the suspension of belief, the utter openness
to experience—one can better understand the near-mystical enthusiasm with which Valéry describes the process of bringing a poem to
the page:

> Try to imagine . . . what the least of our acts implies. Think of every-
> thing that must go on inside a man who utters the smallest intelligible
> sentence, and then calculate all that is needed for a poem by Keats or
> Baudelaire to be formed on an empty page in front of the poet.
>
> Think, too, that of all the arts, ours is perhaps that which co-
> ordinates the greatest number of independent parts or factors: sound,
> sense, the real and the imaginary, logic, syntax, and the double in-
> vention of content and form . . . and all this by means of a medium
> essentially practical, perpetually changing, soiled, a maid of all work,
> *everyday language,* from which we must draw a pure, ideal Voice, capable
> of communicating without weakness, without apparent effort, with-
> out offense to the ear, and without breaking the ephemeral sphere
> of the poetic universe, an idea of some *self* miraculously superior to
> Myself.[15]

"An idea of some *self* miraculously superior to Myself"? Isn't that the thought which Rilke himself had struggled to form when he paced the bastions of Schloss Duino in the winter of 1911? And what Stevens imagined in that "strong exhilaration / Of what we feel from what we think, of thought / Beating in the heart, as if blood newly came, // An elixir, an excitation, a pure power" ("It Must Be Abstract," canto III)?

Once again we come in proximity of angels. For what is Heidegger's unthinkable thought which recedes as we approach it—but an angel? And what is that huge, untouchable loss which Rilke felt more powerfully than his physical life—but an angel? And what are memory? childhood? death? And what, after all, is the unconscious itself —but spaces filled with winged, invisible spirits borne within us, as in dreams? And what in Valéry is that "idea of some *self* miraculously superior to Myself"—but another form of angel? We move among shadows, we move among shades, but from whom or what those presences come remains a lifelong mystery to us. And not to solve that mystery, but to continually think us back to it—to become Stevens's "man who has had time to think enough"—remains an enduring necessity of poetry.

Divine Hunger

A Poetics of Cannibalism

"The teeth in love . . ."
—Lucretius, *De rerum natura*

"You must sit down, sayes Love, and taste my meat."
—George Herbert, "Love"

1

"If a native falls from a tree . . . he is generally killed and eaten."

2

At sixteen, St. Augustine stole an armful of pears from a neighboring orchard, though the sin he confessed was not a theft inspired by his taste for pears—they were a shriveled, worm-eaten lot in any case—but an appetite inspired by his taste for sin: "For if any of these fruit entered my mouth, the sweetener of it was my sin in eating."

3

In the story of the Garden, Eve "took of the fruit thereof, and did eat, and gave also unto her husband with her; and he did eat. And the eyes of them both were opened, and they knew that they were naked; and they sewed fig leaves together, and made themselves aprons."

But far from satisfying a hunger, their small feast exposed a terrible secret—"the appetite grows by eating"—a secret that eventually came to serve as a judgment upon the living: "What is commonly called love, namely the desire of satisfying a voracious appetite with a certain quantity of delicate white human flesh."

4

Less naked in the mirror than she is to us—who, in the late-seventeenth-century fashion, view her discreetly from our place behind—the woman in Velázquez's *Rokeby Venus,* still warm and damp from her morning bath, seems not to be about "the immobility of myth" so much as "some fruitful trace" (Robert Conquest) of who she is. While she regards herself, we regard her from a perspective that reveals "all together, / Face, shoulders, waist, delectable smooth thighs."

In the modern version—Munch, Gorky, Schiele, et al.—a radical change occurs. The reclining figure, no longer viewed as a site of passive contemplation, becomes instead the instinctual field of a ravishment, where craving, voraciousness, gluttony, power will bring to bear the full and ancient prerogatives of hunger. In the modern version, the appetite of a thousand years becomes the subject of what it consumes.

5

At dinner one evening a visiting English anthropologist explains to everyone seated at the table, "Though cannibalism is not confined to humans—a lion might eat lion flesh, for example, and it's also considered a cannibal—only when practiced by humans is it considered beneath the species. Only a human can be *in*human. Only a human can yield to inhumanity."

Later, the coffee and dessert dishes pushed to one side, the informal lecture concluded, he sits back heavily in his chair with the air of a man unhappy to see his appetites end.

But then—as if "out of the eater came forth the meat"—the graduate assistant assigned to him returns from the restroom, her lipstick and hair restored. He appears to watch her with an eager, newly rekindled hunger, and, as with all his earlier observations, everyone at the table sees what he means, indeed it seems we acknowledge it right along with him, the not-altogether-unthinkable fact—figures of speech aside—that she looks truly good enough to eat.

6

"'Then you should say what you mean,' the March Hare went on.

"'I do,' Alice hastily replied; 'at least—at least I mean what I say—that's the same thing, you know.'

"'Not the same thing a bit!' said the Hatter. 'Why, you might just as well say that "I see what I eat" is the same thing as "I eat what I see!"'"

7

Eager to make his new religion more palatable to Mediterraneans, whose pagan rites included animal sacrifice and feasting, the disciple Paul represented Jesus as the Paschal lamb offered up for sacrifice at Passover.

In 1215, Pope Innocent III—no less eager to close that gap which Paul's ingenious metaphor had left between reality and the word—decreed as an absolute article of faith that the bread and wine of the sacrament were no longer figures of speech.

From that day forward, the eating would cease to be symbolic. From that day forward, when one consumes the Host (from the Latin *hostia*, meaning "sacrificial victim"), one consumes, not the figurative, but the literal flesh of Christ.

8

But the story goes back even further. For as Luke has carefully noted, when Christ was born his mother "wrapped him in swaddling clothes, and laid him in a manger." A manger (from the French verb *manger* 'to eat'): a feeding trough for livestock that resembles in shape the modern day crib (from the Old English *cribb* 'a manger'). When Christ was born, he was presented to the world in the symbolic form of fodder, a fact, pagan as it was, borne out in the traditional Christmas crèche (from the Old French *creche* 'a manger, a crib'), where various livestock—whose feeding trough that manger was—now gaze down on him with a soulful, curiously human hunger.

9

It's an ancient struggle, the ongoing effort to refigure in words precisely what, when, and how to eat. Instead of milk, one drinks Agni's semen. Instead of bread and wine, one eats the flesh and blood of Christ. A linguistic sleight-of-hand intended to disguise ("long pig," "two-legged mutton," "Paschal lamb") or to insist on ("the parson's nose," "the nun's thighs," "the nipples of the virgin") specific anthropophagic associations.

Eating, it may be said, is as much a matter of language as it is of the body, so that proscriptions against particular sources of nourishment, and the ritual necessity of others, have more to do with what's good to think (Claude Lévi-Strauss) than what's good to eat. Or, to put it more simply, food becomes food only at that moment we call it food.

10

A woman who, while making love, makes the grunts, growls, yelps, and whimpers of any number of animals. And yet (and so?) if someone were to imitate the particular sound of whatever she's served at mealtime—the *moo* of a cow, the *cluck* of a chicken, the *baa* of a lamb—experiences a nausea so severe she's rendered incapable of eating.

11

"The curious sympathy one feels when feeling with the hand the naked meat . . . of another person's body."

12

History and nature are in agreement here: Only by eating do you become a god (*la grande ardeur*). But it's also true that what the gods envy most deeply in us, what makes them tremble from their seats on high, is that same insatiable hunger that both stimulates and bedevils us. For what is hunger but a reminder of our own mortality—if we do not eat, we die—that difference they cannot possess. That difference which drives us to yearn for, violate, fetishize, hoard those very things we would consume. Hence the more we hunger—"as newborn babes desire the sincere milk of the word"—the riper we are for God.

13
"*Moth:* They have been at a great feast of languages, and stolen the scraps.
"*Costard:* O! They have lived long on the alms-basket of words. I marvel thy master hath not eaten thee for a word."

14
To savor a word, to swallow a lie, to devour a book ("I do not read, I *eat.*"—Simone Weil), a taste or a distaste for the secret diaries of Comte Donatien Alphonse François de Sade.

15
Or Othello's handkerchief steeped in a juice which "the skilful conserved of maidens' hearts."

16
The flesh made word. "I remember, at the age of twelve or thirteen, reading the following sentence: 'The flesh is sad, alas, and I have read all the books' [Mallarmé]. I was struck with astonishment mingled with scorn and disgust. As if a tomb had spoken. What a lie! And beyond, what truth: for the flesh is a book. A Body 'read,' finished? A book— a decaying carcass? Stench and falsity. The flesh is writing, and writing is never read. . . ."

17
The word made flesh. "Some *Bookes* are to be Tasted, Others to be Swallowed, and Some Few are to be Chewed and Digested."

18

"For verily, my brethren, the spirit *is* a stomach!"

19

And the stomach is a grave. Until the mid-1960s, New Guineans viewed the consuming of human flesh as the customary way of caring for the dead. After a deceased family member received a proper mourning, the body was prepared for eating, often with ginger and assorted vegetables, and consumed by the gathered family. Although certain restrictions applied (i.e., so as not to undermine his strength, a husband couldn't eat his wife, though the reverse was perfectly acceptable), on the whole it was considered an efficient way to dispose of the body and preserve the spirit of the deceased.

20

On the other hand, when the body of an enemy was brought to the village, it provided occasion for further acts of aggression: stonings, beatings, mockery, abuse; when a warrior copulated with a female corpse, he was seen to be attacking his enemy.

In one such instance, a warrior was leisurely having his way with a newly-killed female foe when an impatient kinswoman, knife in hand, began cutting out the corpse's belly. Careless with her work, she inadvertently sliced off a piece of the warrior's penis, which she quickly and resourcefully popped into her mouth, thereby preserving both the spirit and ceremonial status of her charge.

21

Along with his proscription against the consuming of human flesh, the Buddha forbade the eating of, among other things, lion, snake, tiger, horse. Curiously, the bull was set aside this list, an exclusion which (ever more curious, since animal sacrifice was forbidden as well) King Asoka upheld when Buddhism was made the state religion some twenty-three hundred years ago.

22

Unlike the Roman god Bacchus, who was associated exclusively with wine, the Greek god Dionysus was considered the incarnation of all the vital fluids—milk, water, sperm, wine—a distinction which deepens when we consider a story from the great god's earliest years:

While still an infant, the son of Zeus was placed in the care of the Titans, who set him at the center of a ring they formed, dancing around him, dancing as though to the lulling rhythms of a nursery rhyme. Initiates all, they were drawn together by a shared responsibility, but also by a crime.

Sensing some danger in store for him (was it the glint off the knife in a Titan's hand?), Dionysus attempted to elude his fate by taking on various alternate forms—among them a lion, snake, tiger, horse, and, at last, a bull. But having lingered too long in this last disguise, he was set upon by the Titans, who cut him into pieces and roasted the *disiecta membra* on a spit. Their feast having come to an end, Zeus hurled down a magnificent thunderbolt which instantly struck the Titans dead.

But why had he waited so long, a reader may well ask? Waited until they'd had their fill of that tender flesh? Was it because he knew that only in the eager satisfaction of their hunger would Dionysus be re-membered?

Whatever the case, a film of soot was all that remained of the Titans. And in the very same way that a plant will spring from the loamy earth, humankind arose from the broadcast shadow of that ash. "Hence the proverbial expressions: 'Titans in us,' 'the Titanic nature of man,'" and the Orphic doctrine that the soul confined in the human body is composed of that Dionysian substance which survived in the Titans' ashes.

23

"The edible plant is not given by Nature: it is the product of an assassination, because that is how it was created at the beginning of time."

24

Adam and Eve had lived in harmony with other animals until they broke the taboo against eating a particular fruit—which, given the fact that apples didn't exist in the ancient Holy Land, was more likely an apricot. Because of their trespass, they were expelled from Eden and condemned to eat bread "in the sweat of thy face." And to eat it until "thou return unto the ground; for out of it wast thou taken: for dust thou art, and unto dust shalt thou return."

25

In ancient Egypt bread was fashioned in the shape of a phallus, and like the phallus it rose and swelled as it baked. In North America, the oven in which the bread is baked is associated with the vagina, from which derives, *by word of mouth*, the slang expression "putting the bread in the oven."

26

History no doubt repeats itself, but only in ritual do those repetitions actually take us at our word: "One day the brothers who'd been driven out came together, killed and devoured their father and so made an end of the patriarchal horde. United, they had the courage to do and succeeded in doing what would've been impossible individually. . . . In the act of devouring him they accomplished their identification, each one acquiring a portion of his strength. The totem meal, mankind's earliest festival, would thus repeat and commemorate this criminal deed, the beginning of so many things—of social organization, of moral restrictions, and of religion."

27

Although cannibalism was widespread in Europe throughout the ninth and tenth centuries, when roving bands of professional killers brought butchered human carcasses to market where they were sold as "two-legged mutton," and though it persisted in Central Europe until well after the Middle Ages, colonial powers frequently cited this "barbarous practice" as license to overthrow tribal societies which often had no history of the practice at all.

The term "cannibal," in fact, derives from the mispronunciation, by Spanish conquistadors, of the name of the Carib people of the West Indies (whom they called "Canibal"). Perhaps the speed with which this term became synonymous with "man-eater" in European languages is one indication of how crucial a role that concept played in preparing the way for that usurpation of priority which the latecomer exerts on all earlier claims.

28

"And of the Cannibals that each other eat,
The Anthropophagi, and men whose heads
Do grow beneath their shoulders. This to hear
Would Desdemona seriously incline."

29

As an indicator of difference, as a way of dominating, stigmatizing and dehumanizing the other, food—or what is designated "food"—has served as a powerful political tool. In fact, the degree to which one feels superior to another people might be gauged by the degree of one's repugnance to their diet.

Like all such imprisoned fictions, this one gave rise to a reality (i.e., *haute cuisine*) and to an abiding cultural principle: "Tell me what thou eatest, and I will tell thee what thou art."

30

The witches' soup in *Macbeth*, for example—that cauldron boil of dog's tongue, bat's wool, eye of newt, lizard's leg, blindworm's sting, and fillet of fenny snake—awakened a profound physical disgust in the genteel Elizabethan audience, a disgust that signified the extent to which they identified themselves with the play's nobility and the lower classes with that throng of hags.

31

Conversely, the Roman Emperor Vitellius was said to prize, as much for the pleasures of reciting the ingredients as for the pungent flavors those ingredients imparted, a dish that was made from peacock brains, pike livers, flamingo tongues, and the sex glands of the lamprey eel.

32

The image-fetish as a basis of power, a power inherent in language, in the belief that someone is "only as good as his word," was something Montaigne recognized early in his study of the Brazilian cannibals: "In order to make their prisoners love life more they treat them generously in every way, but occupy their thoughts with the menaces of the death awaiting all of them, of the tortures they will have to undergo and of the preparations being made for it, of limbs to be lopped off and of the feast they will provide. All that has only one purpose: to wrench some weak or unworthy word from their lips."

33

"And when I looked, behold, an hand was sent unto me; and, lo, a roll [scroll] of a book was therein. . . . Moreover he said unto me, Son of man, eat that thou findest; eat this roll. . . . So I opened my mouth, and he caused me to eat the roll."

34

But where does it end? In the folk history of the Goodenough islands it is recorded that a wise and powerful leader named Malaveyoyo promoted a Modawa festival, a festival held to entice his warring people back from the bush and into the shelter of the village center.

At the end of a year of celebrations, Malaveyoyo distributed bread and pigs to everyone in the surrounding Nibita, a gesture by which he formally declared the warring over and the practice of cannibalism ended. From that day forward, he officially decreed, everyone must put down their weapons, and if they fight at all, they shall only fight with food.

35

At a recent black-tie ceremony in London, the winner of an English literary award stepped to the podium to denounce the corporate sponsor and to pledge his prize money to the Black Panther Party. A gesture which, as reported in the pages of *The New Yorker*, "caused the assembled writers to pound their cutlery and throw bread rolls."

36

The end of cannibalism marks the beginning of the food fight, the transmuted violence of both animal appetite and human ritual—an instinct which appears to exceed the possibilities it envisioned, to pass beyond the limits of nourishment, fulfillment, satiety, and survival. An instinct whose meaning we dare not speak.

37

The face makes visible the mouth, the mouth makes visible the lips, the lips the teeth, the teeth the tongue, the tongue the throat, the throat the passage the soul takes when a "light breath leaves us. . . .

38

. . . and the spirit, / rustling, flitters away."

39

"I dreamed I floated at will in the great Ether, and I saw this world floating also not far off, but diminished to the size of an apple. Then the angel took it in his hand and brought it to me and said, 'This must thou eat.' And I ate the world."

"Into the Unknown to Find the New"

Baudelaire's Voyage

Embarkation

The title of this essay is a rough translation of the closing line of Baudelaire's epochal "Le Voyage," a title, a poem, and a poet I have selected in order to suggest that there is something more than a casual link between that far-flung seascape which lies beyond the doorstep of the Poets' House[1] and the impression I have that poets by nature are drawn to that same ungoverning spirit which fuels the voyager's heart and mind. Moreover, I'd like to suggest that Baudelaire not only refined that compulsion to a degree that anticipates many of the defining issues of our day (it's from Baudelaire, after all, that we're given the term "the modern") but that his particular kind of voyage has radically altered the way we think about poetry today. And so, true to the voyage's ancient summons—to reenter the domain of uncertainty, to invite the unbidden to repossess, hence recreate, our settled lives—I would like to begin with that same spiritual and cultural ambivalence, that same uncharted destiny which, since Baudelaire's day, has impelled our poems through the troubled waters of the modern world. For has there ever been, in any other century, a poetry of such desperate wandering, such unresolved restlessness, such exile, exodus, and expatriation?

But how and where did this particular voyage begin? Several years ago, while living in Paris, I thought I'd stumbled on a clue. I had spent a long autumn afternoon tracking down the address of Baudelaire's apartment at the Hôtel Lauzun, on the Île Saint Louis, a small "island" enclave situated in the middle of the Seine. As I stood below its shuttered windows and gazed across the water to the city, I was struck by a sensation the poet himself must've experienced often on his daily round. For as the river poured past in front of me, I felt as though I were drifting through space, as though the "Île" were a ship steaming through the heart of what Baudelaire saw as the monumental squalor of the modern city. And therein lay an inkling of that sea change he had ushered in, for this ship had no destination: It was headed nowhere, leaving nowhere, cast adrift on a vast urban expanse our century's most celebrated poem declared, once and for all, a wasteland.

In order to understand how unprecedented Baudelaire's voyage was, it's necessary to recall the crisis that was then taking hold in the heart of the Euro-Christian world. In historical as well as literary terms, Baudelaire marks what Heidegger later referred to as "the beginning of the end of the day of the gods." And what lay beyond that beginning was a paralyzing period of in-betweenness ("too late for the gods and too early for Being"), an encircling nullity of unimaginable scale. In "What Are Poets For?" Heidegger set out to describe the impoverishment which in poets our century have been called to face (and in some ways resolve)—but which Baudelaire, in the middle of the nineteenth century, felt called to face alone:

> Night is falling. . . . The evening of the world's age has been declining toward its night . . . and [this] default of God means that no god any longer gathers men and things unto himself, visibly and unequivocally, and by such gathering disposes the world's history and man's sojourn in it. The time of the world's night is the destitute time. . . . It has already grown so destitute, it can no longer discern the default of God as a default.[2]

However overwrought, even febrile that language may sound to us today (like a doomsday prophet with a sandwich board), it wasn't wholly uncharacteristic of the time. Indeed, this selfsame attitude lent our century its distinctly "modern" character and lent our voyage its fatally existential edge. In Heidegger's view we had cast off from the moorings of Western civilization: from a belief in the primacy of reason, the rational structure of nature, the meaningfulness of history, and the traditions of morality, social thought, and art.

But as Baudelaire was first to understand, being unmoored is one thing, being destinationless is another. The first is a condition of the present, the second a condition of the future as well, and in Baudelaire's mind our destiny was to wander aimlessly, unsure of why or where we're going, precisely because there's no longer anywhere to wander to, not even the future. In the Medieval period, for example, the journey's end was always clear. The pilgrims of *The Canterbury Tales*, or *Morte D'Arthur*, or *Sir Gawain and the Green Knight* moved with dogged Christian resolve toward a destination predicated long before their journeys began. But the modern voyager is not a pilgrim; indeed, the very idea of "destination" is thrown into an irreversible doubt. Like the man in Kafka's "The Hunter Gracchus," the modern voyager has already died, and yet, because his "death-ship" has lost its course, he remains among the living: "Nobody will read what I say here, no one will come to help me.... My ship has no rudder and it is driven by the wind that blows in the undermost regions of death."[3]

"Le Voyage" may be read, not only as a paradigm for the condition Heidegger describes, but as the acknowledged prototype for much of what is now called "literary modernism." In its drive to separate the harsh and distinctive reckonings of the voyage from the promised bounty of the voyage's end, Baudelaire anticipates our predilection for process over product, for the means of making over and above what the making means. Long before the supervention of such novelty phrases as "the deferral of meaning," "the refusal of closure,"

or "the poetry of indeterminacy," "Le Voyage" had shouldered in to
question the illusory prospect of arrival:

> The lookout hails each island, after dark,
> as El Dorado and the Promised Land;
> imagination readies for its feast—
> and sights a sandbar by the morning light.
>
> Irons or overboard with the drunken tar,
> pathetic lover of chimerical coasts
> who dreams Atlantis and then finds the sea
> emptier for one more fond mirage!
>
> One more old sailor in the muddy slums
> who meditates, half blind, on Happy Isles
> and thinks he sees the beacons of Dakar
> each time a candle gutters in the dark.[4]

The thrice-repeated drama of those stanzas points up the idea that
the modern voyager yearns, not for somewhere, but for somewhere
else—a Promised Land, Atlantis, the beacons of Dakar—and un-
derscores the idea that such quests all end in the diminished reality
of a burnished sandbar, an empty sea, a candle guttering in the dark.
Only on the voyage itself, it seems, only in that aimless passage between the sureties of boredom and thwarted dreams, does the heart
preserve its "brilliancy": "One hope remains: / to venture forth, with
'Onward!' as our cry."

At this point it may be useful to tailor our vocabulary to suit this
discussion's purposes. First of all, let's call a trip which has a destination a *journey,* and those who take a journey *travelers.* And then, let's
call a trip whose only object is to "leave for leaving's sake" a *voyage,*
and those who take a voyage *voyagers.* With the former, travel is the
obstacle to arrival; with the latter, travel is all of arrival one has. For
the voyager "one hope remains," to experience against the backdrop
of the great unknown that sharp intoxication of not knowing what's
in store for us. The voyager always calls "away," never "toward," af-

firming the desire for a state of being which eradicates both the points
of departure and the imaginary points of arrival:

> some are escaping from their country's shame,
> some from the horror of life at home, and some
> —astrologers blinded by a woman's stare—
> are fugitives from Circe's tyranny;
>
> rather than be turned to swine they drug
> themselves on wind and sea and glowing skies;
> rain and snow and incinerating suns
> gradually erase her kisses' scars.
>
> But only those who leave for leaving's sake
> are [*les vrais voyageurs*]; hearts tugging like balloons,
> they never balk at what they call their fate
> and, not knowing why, keep muttering 'away!'

Considering the facts of Baudelaire's life, the temptation persists
to read that list as an ascending scale of personal miseries: his disgust
with contemporary bourgeois culture, his sense of his desecrated
childhood home, his tormented and often violent relationship with
la Vénus noire, Jeanne Duval. But it's important to note the shift in emphasis from the first two stanzas to the third. In the first two, the reasons for voyaging are consciously formulated—all are fleeing from
some private hell—but *les vrais voyageurs* of stanza three, "not knowing why," simply "leave for leaving's sake."

This sudden shift from conscious revulsion to a generalized, almost mindless impulse to dispossess expressly anticipates the rudder-
less wanderings of "the modern." For Baudelaire finally perceived
himself not as someone who actually chose his life—and who therefore could choose to escape it—but as someone in whom a life had
formed. It was an inner spiritual sickness that drove him wildly
"round and round / like a sun some cruel Angel spins in space" (section 2). *But at least he knew it as a sickness.* That the rest of the world did
not explains why his poems, even from our far remove in time, remain
so freakishly apocalyptic.

The Poem as Voyage

"So what are poets for in a destitute time?" Heidegger asks. Certainly each age needs its poets to help define the distinctive nature of its times, but if that were poetry's only function it would long ago have lost its place to the philosophers, historians, and social scientists. For poetry is always something more, and something other, than its subject. It is subject (matter) made energy (verb), and in that sense it provides not just a conceptual basis for our collective voyage, but the visceral experience of the voyage itself. By the curve of its own subversive logic, poetry refuses both the tyranny of arrival (summary, paraphrase, reducible meaning) and the easy consolations of credulity (the conviction that would separate sound from sense)—in Baudelaire's phrase, poetry remains a quest "whose goal cannot be known."

This distinction between *idea* and *experience*, between *meaning* and *being*—or, if you will, between the *journey* and the *voyage*—becomes clearer in Valéry's famous comparison of poetry and prose. In his essay "Poetry and Abstract Thought," he advances the argument that poetry is to prose what dancing is to walking, a contention one might illustrate as follows.

You walk to the store to buy a bottle of milk, and when the milk is purchased the walk is forgotten. You've exchanged the potential adventure of walking for the foreknown object of the walk. The case, Valéry maintains, is similar with prose, whose purpose is to arrive at a meaning, or to persuade of a truth, or to convey some information; and once that end is accomplished, you needn't relive the excursion.

With the dance, on the other hand, there is no object beyond the dance, beyond the physical experience of the body's movement. The adventure of the dance is its one and only object, and the only way of possessing that object is to repeat the dance exactly as before. This, Valéry claims, is equally the case with poetry: "The poem . . . doesn't die for having lived, it is expressly designed to be born again from its ashes and to become endlessly what it has just been. . . . It stimulates us to reconstruct it identically." [5]

By our earlier definitions, prose represents a *journey*, a means to an end, a process of arrival; poetry, on the other hand, represents a *voyage*, a process which has no external goal, or whose only goal is to endlessly become "what it has just been." Where the energy of the journey is linear, the energy of the voyage is systolic and diastolic.

Of course, these distinctions aren't truly genre-bound. Comparing, for example, two of Hopkins's devotional poems we encounter similar distinctions. In the last lines of "Pied Beauty"—a poem of early self-assurance and faith—one gets the impression, suggested in part by the offhand compliance of its parenthetic phrase, that the poem too knowingly leads us to expect the solid landfall of its final line:

> All things counter, original, spare, strange;
>> Whatever is fickle, freckled (who knows how?)
>>> With swift, slow; sweet, sour; adazzle, dim;
>> He fathers-forth whose beauty is past change:
>>>>> Praise him.

But with "Carrion Comfort"—believed to be the sonnet "written in blood" in those anguished years before Hopkins's death—one feels that certainty thrown into question, one feels the poem's noncompliance, its inwrought refusal to cede its doubt (signaled in part by the shocked incredulity of *its* parenthetic phrase) as the basis for its unswerving power:

> Cheer whom though? The Hero whose heaven-handling flung me,
>> fóot tród
> Me? or me that fought him? O which one? is it each one? That
>> night, that year
> Of now done darkness I wretch lay wrestling with (my God!)
>> my God.

Like Cézanne's celebrated oranges, tipped by the table's altered scale, the pitched uncertainty of those lines—will the poet's faith slide irreversibly into unbelief? will wretchedness replace what once was praise?—lends the poem an abiding tension, a withheld outcome that conveys some feeling for the terrible struggle his faith entailed. Where "Pied Beauty" remains comforting and, for the believer, reassuring (as arrivals and certainties tend to be), "Carrion Comfort" proves disturbing and unresolved—it sends us back to the strained intensities of the lookout.

Am I suggesting, then, that the poem of belief is inherently less interesting, or less "modern," than the poem of doubt? I hope not, for of course in lyric poetry what is or isn't interesting is always a matter of the words themselves, of how accurately they represent the inner life of the speaker—regardless of their conviction. But by that same measure, "Carrion Comfort" makes, for me, the more compelling and credible "religious" poem precisely because, when I set the two poems aside, it is (paradoxically) the passionate incertitude, more than the exuberant praise, that makes the possibility of faith a more accessible part of my inner life. The degree to which this remains a function of the contingencies mentioned above is, of course, a matter for the individual reader to decide.

Vehicle, Terrain, Domain

So what, exactly, is at stake in the voyage—what must be risked? what can be gained?—and how essential is that stake to the voyage's success? At the simplest level, what are the requisite elements that give a voyage its identity? What do those elements tell us, and how do we come to know them? And since I've attempted to link the two, to what extent can poetry be extrapolated through the properties of a voyage?

To begin with, every voyage requires a *vehicle*, a mode of transport—a "sailing vessel," whether ocean frigate or poetry's wing, the body's yearnings (desire, hunger, our capacity for love) or the human mind (memory, reflection, imagination, dream). Second, every voyage requires a *terrain* over which the voyager must pass, and that terrain, as we know from Homer's wine-dark sea, is over-swept by the whisper of death. Peril, whether physical, psychological, spiritual, or sexual, peril pervades its element—hence every voyage is potentially the last. And third, every voyage requires a *domain* into which the voyager enters, and the identifying feature of that domain is the siren-call to come out of ourselves. We arrive in this world, as Simone Weil has observed, with only one belonging, that frail, interior, shadow-self "I"; and yet no human experience is more blissful, more fraught with joy, than that which comes from surrendering the I . . . through love, through the ardors of religion, through our passionate attachments to the natural world.

Vehicle, terrain, domain . . . But even as we pronounce those terms, we sense some anterior concept which none of those terms takes into account. For it seems impossible to think about a voyage without first considering "home," that place from which all voyages are launched. Even for earlier periods, it's easy enough to think about a voyage without considering its destination—after all, one can always turn around and go back, or one can always travel full circle, or one can always lose oneself along the way. But one can't begin to think about a voyage without first considering the point of departure.

And what is that point, in all our many and various voyages, what is that point except "home"? Without Penelope and Ithaca, how foolishly idealistic Odysseus's voyage would seem; without Christianity, how remote the idea of a spreading dark might sound to us today; without our own cultivated memories of childhood, how dully uninformed the leavening experiences of adulthood become. Whatever we might claim for them, however liberating we'd like them to be, all voyages retain (all voyages cast) the dark penumbra of home.

In fact, among other more exacting claims, it may be said that the voyage is an attempt to locate and affix some morally functional pathos of home. On the one hand we have the long-standing contention (with its basis in Homer) that the voyage provides the only possible pathway home; on the other hand we have the counter contention (with its modern basis in Freud) that the voyage leads to a partial restitution for the irrevocable loss of home.

A third alternative, a darker one, the one Baudelaire appears to have chosen, suggests that the voyage functions to keep us from ever having to return home. After all, the terrors of the voyage are small when we consider, as Baudelaire did, that the greatest pains are inflicted at home. Fate—we can endure enormous suffering at the hands of fate —but how unendurable when suffering derives from the hands of those we love. The perils of the voyage (*death, uncertainty, dissolution, loss*) are defined in advance by the broken promises of home (*safety, trust, formation, hope*), the locus of those raw, originative traits which drive our voyages like a heavy wind. In one of many paradoxes in his life, Baudelaire's quest for love was launched *away* from the very place where it should be found.

Perhaps this explains why Baudelaire's biography takes on such profound allegorical significance. By most accounts his turbulent inner voyage—Sartre remarked that "his one and only voyage seems to have been a long torment"—was mapped out in the fraught circumference of home, in that fateful year (he was six at the time) that his father died and his mother remarried the imposing Captain Aupick—"an incurable wound," as Baudelaire described it. In his rooms in later life he had hung unframed and nailed to the wall the series prints of Delacroix's *Hamlet*; and he was often to remark, "When one has a son like me, one doesn't remarry." This rupture in the sheltering life of the home would register itself on Baudelaire's mind as a permanent dispossession; or, as Sartre described it in his psychoanalytical study of the poet, it released Baudelaire

> into a personal existence without any warning or preparation. One moment he was still enveloped in the communal religious life of the couple consisting of his mother and himself; the next life had gone out like a tide leaving him high and dry. The justification for his experience had disappeared; he made the mortifying discovery that he was a single person, that his life had been given him for nothing.[6]

The personal crisis Baudelaire endured reflects, in kind, the spiritual crisis this century has faced. More importantly for us—the future beneficiaries of the art by which he transmuted that crisis—the anguish he suffered privately, in the guises of son and lover, he embodied publicly, in the guises of poet and aesthetician. Certainly his lifelong obsession with that one dimension of experience contributes to his fascination as a poet. And perhaps to his limitation. But as Heidegger observed, "It is a necessary part of the poet's nature that, before he can be truly a poet in such an age [as ours], the time's destitution must have made the whole being and vocation of the poet a poetic question for him."[7] And for that Baudelaire appeared to possess an indefatigable genius.

Home

But what is home? a reader may well ask. How is it composed? To what urgings in us does it respond? How do we come to define it? And, more significantly, how does it come to define us? To sketch out an answer, I've selected a few phrases from Gaston Bachelard's *The Poetics of Space*, phrases which summon the more elemental features of that place: a "protected intimacy"; "an attachment that is native in some way"; an "essential, sure, immediate well-being"; "a primitiveness which belongs to all, rich and poor alike"; "the non-I that protects the I"; "the original shell."

What we hear in those phrases, and in the passage to follow, is a gradually accruing value of space, a layering like the oyster's pearl around the grain of sand, a value that, once fully formed, is stowed somewhere in the subterranean storehouse of memory and dreams: "The old saying: 'We bring our *lares* with us' has many variations. . . . Memories of the outside world will never have the same tonality as those of home and, by recalling these memories, we add to our store of dreams; we are never real historians, but always near poets, and our emotion is perhaps nothing but an expression of a poetry that was lost."[8]

So, then, what does it mean to lose, or to leave, that space? Certainly it doesn't mean that the space is somehow erased from memory—quite the contrary. In Baudelaire's case it meant he eventually perceived that space not as something *he* had abandoned, but as something that had abandoned *him*. And like many a spurned lover, his anguish proved directly proportionate to the depth of his attachment.

We get some feeling for the gravity of that attachment in "L'invitation au voyage," a poem composed five years before its more famous counterpart. Barbara Johnson has written an illuminating essay about the self-enclosed, infantile world that Baudelaire actually wishes for when he invites the reluctant lover of the poem (whom he addresses, significantly, as "*my sister, my child*") to voyage with him to a faraway place "where even the landscape *resembles you*"; where "all would whisper / to the soul in secret / the sweet *mother tongue*"; where "*All is order* . . . and elegance, / pleasure, peace, and opulence" (my italics). Sound familiar? As Baudelaire had earlier argued in an essay on Banville, "Any lyric poet, by his very nature, inevitably brings about a return to the lost Eden."

Eden, origin, incest. Each suggests its own and yet a similar kind of leveling. Each involves the symbolic elimination of difference. Each involves an imaginary place where all is *luxe, calme et volupté*. Imaginary *and* ideal (as our images of home tend to be) because in such a place the *I* is no longer different from *you*, the self and the other are one and the same—hence one is never alone. When Baudelaire discovered the bewildering impossibility of that return—to God, the womb, the familial/familiar—he ceased to be a nineteenth-century poet, and in the depths of his soul he registered the horror of being *outside, other, estranged*, of being permanently *different from you*. And in the exquisite agony of that recognition he sounded an imperative which thirty years later a boy in Charleville named Arthur Rimbaud would take up like a fallen flag: "One must be absolutely modern." And what could that mandate possibly mean, except: one must be utterly homeless, one must be utterly alone?

"O Death, Old Captain"

So what are poets for in a destitute time? To give voice to that destitution, yes, but also, and more importantly, to make palpable to us the thinking and feeling experience of destitution. For according to Heidegger, without that experience we will never be able, first, to "discern the 'default of God' as a default" and, second, to begin the process of preparing the ground for some possible future abode. Given the great but moribund achievements of the modern poets, it would appear that it's the second of these steps that poets now, at the beginning of the twenty-first century, are called upon to consider. The step toward a new conception of home.

That Baudelaire took the first of these steps so far in advance of others accounts perhaps for the enormous resistance he encountered in his day. He was the only poet to reject as useless the then-current revival of classicism, and he may have been the first to insist, as he did in an essay on Constantin Guys, that all our originality comes from "the stamp which the times impress on our senses." The necessity for such a contemporary outlook may be summed up in Heidegger's claim that, in times of destitution, "there must be mortals who reach sooner into . . . *where* the danger is"; and "where that happens we may assume poets to exist who are on the way to the destiny of the world's age."

How clearly Baudelaire was on that path may be determined in part by the traces of his work that are countlessly played through the works of those writers who staked out the territory of "modernism": Eliot, Céline, Rhys, Beckett, Conrad, Sartre, Genet . . . to name just a few. From the vast remove of the nineteenth century, Baudelaire foresaw a world that would imagine art, in Picasso's famous phrase, as "a hoard of destructions," and in his own no less memorable phrase, as "le spectacle ennuyeux de l'immortel péché" ("a wretched pageant of immortal sin"). A world in which one takes for granted the tyranny of politics, the monotony of religion, the corruption of men and women. To read "Le Voyage" in light of its time is to hear that world coming into being like the grinding of historical tectonic plates.

By the end of "Le Voyage" this nightmare finds solution only in that same swelling of desire we hear in the poem's opening stanzas. In a world where meaningful destinations have proven false, it's not surprising (though it is, among other things, suicidally bleak) that Death becomes the one unimpeachable hope:

> Just as once we set sail for Cathay,
> wind in our hair, eyes on the open sea,
>
> we shall embark upon the Sea of Shades
> with all the elation of a boy's first cruise.

The details of Baudelaire's harrowing death are well known now, but it may be worth recalling them in light of his efforts to rebuild that home from which he'd been debarred—a home built not of mud and brick, but of guilt and self-laceration. For what do those efforts tell us about the poet who, at forty-six, lay folded in the arms of his mother, struck by the loss of the power of words, stilled by general paralysis and a softening of the brain? Had he found that space which achieved at last a return to the "original shell"? That first communal order of silence? A reabsorption into the universe of one? Was Baudelaire's slow, self-eradicating death the realization of his return to Eden? Or was it instead the dismantling of all he'd labored to build? (For days following Baudelaire's death, his mother would boast that "the author of *Les Fleurs du Mal* had died a Christian.") As one early letter had fatefully noted: "There is something more serious . . . than physical suffering—it's the fear of seeing one's admirable poetic faculty, the clarity of one's ideas and the power of hope, which in reality are my capital, become used up, disintegrate, and disappear." [9]

Like the last section of "Le Voyage," the story of Baudelaire's life hangs poised between a governing purpose and an intractable doubt, between a belief in the redemptive power of poetry and a fear that the modern soul exists in a state of eternal isolation. Looking back on him from our vantage point, he seems in some clairvoyant way to have witnessed the modern world even before its arrival.

How alone he was on that voyage grows all the more striking when we stop to consider that, in the year he was born (1821), Keats would die at twenty-five following what one biographer calls "a harrowing sea voyage" from England; that Shelley was twenty-eight and had just written "To a Skylark," one year before his death by drowning when his open boat was caught in a storm off Leghorn; that Melville was only two years old, twenty years before he first set sail on the whaling ship *Acushnet;* and that it was exactly one hundred years before a man named T. S. Eliot, recovering from nervous exhaustion in Lausanne, would complete the drafts of an epoch-making modernist poem he'd audaciously call *The Waste Land.*

When we think of Baudelaire at twenty-one, smack in the first half of the nineteenth century, composing *Les Fleurs du Mal*—we begin to see how far his poems have traveled, and how urgent the message they brought to the banks of our century. By the time the poems of that ill-starred sibyl had reached the ears of the modern poets, they must have sounded like the belated conscience of their age:

> Amer savoir, celui qu'on tire du voyage!
> Le monde, monotone et petit, aujourd'hui,
> Hier, demain, toujours, nous fait voir notre image:
> Une oasis d'horreur dans un désert d'ennui!
>
> (It is a bitter truth our voyages teach!
> Tiny and monotonous, the world
> has shown—will always show us—what we are:
> oases of fear in the wasteland of ennui!)

À la Recherche de la
Poésie Perdue

~~~~~

Poetry and Translation

It seems that not too long ago, in that walled garden of a simpler age, there were certain assumptions about the time-honored practice of literary translation that were largely taken for granted. In our century, so suspicious of received ideas, not only have those assumptions been called into question, but the very nature of translation itself has been thrown into serious doubt. The walls are down, and the tenured barbarians (to borrow a phrase) are tromping through the flowerbeds.

Or so it's often perceived. Nevertheless, the fact remains that no other period in American poetry has been as deeply influenced by translation, nor as busily set on producing it, as the one we currently inhabit. With varying degrees of self-consciousness, translators continue to assert their claims on our composite poetic character. Particular mannerisms brought over by translation have established themselves as independent styles, congruent with literary invention. Still others have rapidly made their way into the bloodstream of American literature, where they proliferate to the point we barely recognize them for what they are: the rich transfusions of an Other. No longer simply bringing lilacs from a dead land, mixing memory and desire, translators have taken their project to the heart of literary creation.

To understand fully the role translation plays in our culture, one must first consider what orthodoxies are toppled and constructed in its name, and what possibilities for its current practice are preserved and prohibited by those laborers in the trade. Furthermore, one must consider the degree to which we each possess our own uniquely self-constructed imaginations, and the degree to which we are clustered translations of forces wholly external to us. How much of us is a life (original), and how much of us is an afterlife (translation)?

For clearly each of us is, to a large if not exclusive sense, the genetic translation of our biological parents; the psychological translation of our childhoods; the social translation of our race, gender, and class; the emotional translation of our loves and losses, fears and joys, transgressions and personal betrayals. Added to that we are, whether by stubborn resistance or willing assimilation, the living translation of our literary culture, our reading, our generational disavowals and enthusiasms, our institutional poetry organizations, the editorial boards of our literary journals, our real and imagined readers. It may be that much of what we call "sensibility" is less the expression of a fixed identity than the translation of factors external to us.

This subject assumes added significance when thrown into the field of current debate about language and its "meanings." For however clearly we can gauge the accuracy with which a rendering brings forward the selected thematic features of the original, we must still confront the issue of its "feeling," its value as an aesthetic experience, which "meaning" alone cannot ensure. To put it more simply, the linguistic elements of a poem invariably fall short of explaining its metalinguistic effects, and accuracy is only accurate in a limited sense.

Suffice it to say that in matters of translation poetry proves a conundrum. And like the *boule de neige* a touch disturbs into a swirl of animate life, the thinking translation sets in motion soon calls up those nagging theoretical arguments against which poetry in our skeptical age uneasily stakes its claim: the issue of textual authority, translation's part in maintaining the literary canon, translation as a site where cultural codes are scuttled or maintained, the politics of transmission, language's dark indeterminate heart. With what may seem surprising particularity, translation readily engages these issues; and since, by nature, it is bounded by the condition of belatedness, it grounds these issues in the material contexts of time, memory, and tradition.

Just as the rarefied combination of lemon tea and madeleine cakes can summon up the past from the deep reservoir of Marcel's memory, so too the rousing synesthesia of a translator's words can summon up poetry from deep within what Wordsworth called "the vast empire of human society." In the literal sense, translation carries on the search for a lost poetry, for a poetry from which, for one reason or another, we are currently estranged; and in the literary sense, translation simulates a sensory recollection, a body-memory of poetries past. In both cases, translation descends into the shadowy underworld of *what's-no-longer-here,* and its Orphic charge is to bring that poetry back into the light of the upper air.

But poetry, we're told, gets lost in translation. That, like Eurydice, it can't survive the translator's gaze. For all its quotability, Frost's apothegm may be more complex than it first appears, or than Frost himself intended: he went on to say, less ambiguously, "It is also what is lost in interpretation."

But while the general impression has it that a rendering is, by definition, the poetic inferior of the original, even common sense would seem to suggest things aren't as simple as that. For is a translator somehow ethically bound to work as hard as possible to make a translation, not only as good as the original, but also no better? And given a brilliant translator and a minor text, couldn't a rendering actually exceed the original? In his preface to the second edition of *Lyrical Ballads,* Wordsworth applies a similar logic to the act of original creation:

> As it is impossible for the Poet to produce upon all occasions language as exquisitely fitted for the passion as that which the real passion itself suggests, it is proper that he should consider himself as in the situation of a translator, who does not scruple to substitute excellencies of another kind for those which are unattainable by him; and endeavors occasionally to surpass his original, in order to make some amends for the general inferiority to which he feels that he must submit.[1]

So what's to say that in a translated text "excellencies of another kind" can't surpass the "excellencies"—and hence the poetry—of the original?

But then Frost's maxim doesn't say that a translation is necessarily a lesser poem. What it says is that "poetry"—some specifiable quality that exists in the original—gets lost in the process of carrying it over from one language into another. And if, for Frost, poetry amounts to a particular combination of sounds which collectively suggest a particular set of feelings, images, and ideas—what he called "the sound of sense"—then of course you can't alter those particular sounds (however faithful you are to the images, feelings, and ideas) without fundamentally altering that effect we refer to as "poetry." And since any poem's effect depends, by nature, on the preservation of its verbal uniqueness, on the degree of its resistance to a reducible meaning, then you can't have *the poem* in any other words than those of the original.

Which is not to say that you can't have *a poem*, another poem, which attempts to carry across—through a figuring-forth of images, rhetorical levels, schematic and associative uses of sound—something like that original effect. In that sense translation becomes a kind of metaphor for the original, and, as such, it opens itself to the same aesthetic criteria, the same independent evaluation, that any original poem would. To put it another way, even while conceding that poetry is what is lost in translation, one might just as easily assert the opposite: *Poetry is what is gained in translation.* In his essay "The Presence of Translation," Charles Tomlinson, the editor of *The Oxford Book of Verse in English Translation,* recounts the story of a twentieth-century Hungarian poet who, when asked to name the most beautiful poem in his language, replied, "Shelley's 'Ode to the West Wind' in the translation of Árpád Tóth." [2]

Given these concerns, perhaps we can dispense altogether with the notion of translation as a process of verbal substitutions, of simply finding linguistic equations between languages. Instead, we might think of translation, not as a thing unto itself, not as the product of some literary activity, but as a process that begins well before the act itself. "Reading is already translation," the philosopher Hans-Georg Gadamer has remarked, "and translation is translation for the second time."[3] Likewise, each individual language is subject to the internal translations of time: What once was fresh suddenly seems hackneyed, what once was current now seems archaic. A writer's style may soon obscure a writer's words (the case with Swinburne, for example, to many modern readers), and a writer's words may soon dissolve beneath the shifting conventions of the mother tongue. When we encounter *en face* copies of folio and modern versions of Shakespeare's *Sonnets,* we are in some sense dealing with translation, with the shifting iconology of language.

And while time conspires to translate language, it conspires as well to translate the individual writer. When Wordsworth in the 1850 *Prelude* omits from the 1805 version over three hundred lines recounting the story of his affair with Annette Vallon (told through the characters of Vaudracour and Julia), has he not performed an act of translation? Has he not attempted to "carry across," to render for posterity, a version of himself as a young man that was more reflective of himself as an old man? Time and again one sees that process in the 1850 version, where the inspired elaborations of youth are studiously translated, for better or worse, by the measured intellectual purposes of age. Consider this sentence from book IV of the 1805 *Prelude*—

> A wild, unworldly-minded youth, given up
> To Nature and to books, or, at the most,
> From time to time, by inclination shipped,
> One among many, in societies,
> That were, or seemed, as simple as myself.

—and compare it to the same sentence as it appears in the 1850 version:

> A wild, unworldly-minded youth, given up
> To his own eager thoughts.[4]

Or consider the more recent example of Adrienne Rich, who, abandoning her allegiance to the formal structures of her early verse, set out to pursue her "dream of a common language." Was this not a form of translation, an attempt to write in "another language," a language accessible to, and expressive of, the nonliterary reader? And when Robert Lowell, for not so wholly dissimilar reasons, makes a radical departure from the muscular, baroque, allusive pyrotechnics of his early poems to come of age in the lapidary artlessness of *Life Studies*—was that not a form of translation as well?

◆

According to *Webster's*, the word "translate" comes to us from the Middle English *translaten* 'to transport' and from the Latin *translatus* (the past participle of *transferre* 'to carry across'), made up by combining *trans-* (across) + *-latus* (carried). As a transitive verb its primary meaning is "to express in another language, systematically retaining the original sense." A secondary meaning: "To put in simpler terms; explain." A third: "To convey from one form or style to another; convert." A fourth: "To forward or retransmit (a telegraphic message)." A fifth comes from theology: "To convey to heaven without natural death." And a final meaning, archaic now: "to transport; enrapture."

In each case, translation harks back to its expressive, interpretive, telepathic roots, its mysteries of preservation and conveyance, its Ovidian affinity for metamorphosis and change. But where does that impulse come from, the impulse which first gave rise to the word? As is often the case, such secrets are contained in a story, a story imbedded in the living culture, a story very like this one:

In the beginning there was in the whole world only one language, and within that language there were very few words, so that all who spoke were understood by others. For as long as anyone could remember, people had drifted from place to place in camps of wandering tribes. But one year, as migrations to the east led to a plain in the land of Shinar, the tribes decided to join together and build a city, and in that city

they would raise a tower whose spire extended all the way to heaven. In the lofty ac-
complishment of their goal, they would establish an enduring name for themselves,
and no longer would they be scattered like leaves across the face of the earth.

Having come down from above to observe this city with its celebrated, high-reach-
ing tower, the Lord became suspicious, and he began to wonder if perhaps this was
only the beginning of a dream that would, in time, exceed the limitations he had set
for humankind: "Behold," he said, "they are one people, and they have all one lan-
guage; and this is only the beginning of what they will do; and nothing that they pro-
pose to do will now be impossible for them. Come, let us go down, and there confuse
their language, that they may not understand one another's speech."

As the Lord foresaw, His stern command brought on such confusions that the
people of the earth were forced to abandon their city. And as they trailed out in their
separate tribes, confined to the solitude of their separate tongues, they were scattered
like leaves across the face of the earth. It was then that the city was given the name of
Babel, for it was there that God confused the language by which people once under-
stood each other.

And so translation begins with a story—a story which carries within
it the enduring belief in an original language, an *Ursprache*, a language
by which, at some far-off point in our evolution, we once all understood each other. A story which carries the unspoken belief that language contains the essential unifying element of community, and that
human history is the history of language, and that language is a power
that serves to divide those whom it originally united.

Translation, then—that carrying across from one solitude to another—is both the expression of an ancient belief in a common language, and an activity through which we affirm that belief by enacting the means to embody it. To put it in terms of the Genesis story,
translation attempts to restore that original city, to re-imagine that
place where everyone was welcome and everyone was understood.
When the tribes were dispersed from Babel, they left in the isolation
of their individual languages, but they also left with a dream: the
dream of reclaiming that first community, that common language
from which they'd been debarred. Translation begins in the radical

human impulse to contravene, however covertly and however fore-doomed, a direct command of God.

As Wordsworth wrote in a passage apposite to the Babel story:

> In spite of difference of soil and climate, of language and manners, of laws and customs: in spite of things silently gone out of mind, and things violently destroyed; the Poet binds together by passion and knowledge the vast empire of human society, as it is spread over the whole earth, and over all time.[5]

•

But we're an age suspicious of "origins," not to mention of "community"—whose community, we reflexively ask, and founded on what ideological principles?—and before we'll grant much credence to a story like the one we find in Genesis, we'll more likely insist that all is translation and that there's no such thing as an original. In her introduction to *The Art of Translation,* the poet and translator Rosanna Warren makes a more culturally acceptable, and more politically expedient, case for the necessity of translation. "The psychic health of an individual," she explains, "resides in the capacity to recognize and welcome the 'Other'":

> The same could be said of civilization. Our word "idiot" comes from the Greek [*idiotes*], . . . whose primary sense is of privacy, peculiarity, isolation. A person or culture guarding its privacy to an extreme extent becomes "idiotic," even autistic, and such resistance to the foreign, such incapacity to translate, spells its doom. . . . As George Steiner suggests in chapter upon chapter of *After Babel,* from the neurophysiological level on up through the broadest layers of culture, translation of one kind or another guarantees our shared survival.[6]

If an ongoing exposure to the foreign is essential to our survival, then the history of a culture resides in the record of its openness to the other, of its willingness to make itself receptive to, and affected by, those internal conversions which the foreign inspires. This serves, of course, as a caution to xenophobes of whatever stripe, though a culture's willingness to renew its own past is as much a part of that process as its willingness to receive what is geographically and linguistically foreign.

Knowingly or not, translation precipitates an ongoing negotiation between self and other, and this ability to shield oneself from—or to impose oneself on, or to assimilate into oneself—the identity of the other is the ability to be political. And however potent a political role translation plays in a culture, the process itself isn't limited to its most recognizable forms. In the extraordinary case of a poet like Phillis Wheatley, for example, that negotiation between self and other was manifest in more clandestine ways.

Abducted from Africa when she was ten and sold into slavery in Boston, Wheatley became, in 1773, at the age of twenty, the first African American to publish a book of imaginative literature, a collection of poetry modestly entitled *Miscellaneous Poems*. Given the fact that Wheatley's poems adopted a style that imitates Western neoclassical conventions, a "style" so estranged from her own nativity—estranged by at least the three removes of language, race, and culture—the terms of translation readily apply.

Indeed her "translations" were so successful that the white reading public regarded them with either suspicion or outright disbelief: either these were the curious product of some sideshow freak, or testimony to our culture's godly power to domesticate "a savage soul," or, more likely, evidence of some clever literary forgery. Whatever the case, the level of doubt was such that the publisher felt compelled to preface the publication with a note, signed by eighteen of "the most respectable characters in Boston," attesting to the book's "authenticity": "We, whose names are under-written, do assure the World, that the Poems specified in the following page were (as we verily believe) written by Phillis, a young Negro girl, who was but a few years since brought an uncultivated barbarian from Africa."[7]

Wheatley has often been criticized for adopting a style that signifies an indifference to her people's bondage. But things aren't always as simple as they seem. And one of the more remarkable achievements of her work is how it manages, through a complex process of "self-translation," to focus attention on its "recognizable" literary features—a diversion which in turn made possible protests that, in another "language," would have been silenced altogether. In her elegy "On the Death of General Wooster," for example, Wheatley manages to ventriloquize—through the person of General Wooster, a hero of the War of Independence—her claims for the freedom of her people:

> But how, presumptuous shall we hope to find
> Divine acceptance with th' Almighty mind—
> While yet (O deed Ungenerous!) they disgrace
> And hold in bondage Afric's blameless race?
> Let Virtue reign—And thou accord our prayers
> Be victory ours, and generous freedom theirs.

By "translating" her protests into a culturally "acceptable" literary language, into poems that serve as a verbal equivalent of the Trojan horse, Wheatley secreted into that culture an army of ideas radically at odds with its purposes.

◆

If one finds at least minimal historical agreement around the claim that translation transports cultural values from one language to another, one encounters broad disagreement about the methods, responsibilities, and authority to which the translator is entitled. That disagreement, so hotly contested in the critical arenas of the last half-century, has dramatically altered the terms by which we identify the practice today. The traditional cartoon version of the translator portrays a dutiful soul, thesaurus at one side, bilingual dictionary at the other, plodding forward word by word, struggling to keep the transfer accurate. It appears, to be sure, a selfless labor, subordinate to the original author's and, as such, warily monitored by the virtues of "loyalty" on the one hand, the vices of "libertinage" on the other.

Historically associated with the feminine—translation was the sole means women had, beginning in the European Middle Ages, to gain access to the forms of public expression—the translator traditionally occupied a place of discursive inferiority: the author/male holding an elevated position above the translator/female. As a well-known translator of Molière has remarked, translation "is an art, though a very modest minor one," and he goes on to compare the translator's sensitivity to that of the book lover, "whose gifts for good creation or analysis may be modest or nonexistent."

Given the long history of such associations, it's no surprise that the vocabulary of literary translation remains laden with sexual tropes and with a persistently sexist vocabulary. We speak of translations as being "faithful" or "unfaithful," we speak of their "fidelity" or "infidelity" to an original, we speak of them, in one of the more enduring tropes, as "les belles infidèles," as mistresses who can't be both beautiful and faithful at once. As G. K. Chesterton put it, speaking of FitzGerald's translation of *The Rubáiyát*, "It is too good a poem to be faithful to the original." We speak of translations as though there existed between translator and author a pact whose terms of relation, and whose codes of behavior, could be mediated through the conventions of the bourgeois marriage—men produce, women reproduce. Indeed this is one of many crises contemporary translation has encountered. As the critic Barbara Johnson has observed: "The crisis in marriage and the crisis in translation are identical. For while both translators and spouses were once bound by contracts to love, honor, and obey, and while both inevitably betray, the current questioning of the possibility and desirability of conscious mastery makes that contract seem deluded and exploitative from the start."[8] The degree to which a translator feels licensed to interact with the original—to serve as a co-equal in authorship— and the degree to which the translation stands in equivalence to the original, remain defining points in this dispute.

In *The Poem Itself* Stanley Burnshaw argues that the poem's language always holds the higher ground. A translation "takes the reader away from the foreign literature and . . . into something different. The instant he departs from the words of the original, he departs from *its* poetry."[9] The degree to which Burnshaw resists that departure leads him to suggest that the one truly meaningful way to experience a poem in another language is to study that language well enough to make some sense of its sounds. Having accomplished that, one then reads along with the original, using as many commentaries as possible, a process the translator supplements with such helpful pointers as "English approximations (usually set in italics, with alternate meanings in parenthesis and explanations in brackets)," and "comments on allusion, symbol, meaning, sound, and the like." The translator's role, custodial to the privileged status of the original, removed from that dynamic interchange between text and reader, devolves to a purely pedagogical function: to instruct, annotate, and shepherd.

For Walter Benjamin—whose 1923 essay "The Task of the Translator" remains a seminal modernist text on translation—the distinction between poet and translator resides not in value but *intentio:* "The intention of the poet is spontaneous, primary, manifest," while the intention of the translator is "derivative, ultimate, ideational." [10] The poet struggles to bring into language something that exists outside of language, some real or imagined urgency, some emotion or passion or experience. The translator, on the other hand, makes no special claim to that impulse, makes no pretense of ownership, and in any case does not suppose that the impulse itself is excerptable from the language by which it's formed. Rather than subordinating the translator's role to that of the poet, Benjamin regards these distinctions as the basis for its elevation:

> While a poet's words endure in his own language, even the greatest translation is destined to become part of the growth of its own language and eventually to perish with its renewal. Translation is so far removed from being the sterile equation of two dead languages that of all literary forms it is the one charged with the special mission of watching over the maturing process of the original language and the birth pangs of its own. [11]

Their historical relationships aside, Benjamin argues, all languages are interrelated by the way they *intend* their object, so that the value of translation lies not in the transmission of some essential meaning or form but in the effect it has on both the original and the second language. In that sense, the translator assists in the *becoming* of language by enacting "the central reciprocal relationship between languages." This kinship leads Benjamin to conjecture about the futural possibility of a pure language—*die reine Sprache*—a language which "no single language can attain . . . but is . . . that which is meant in all languages." Like Mallarmé's "supreme language," the one Benjamin envisions resembles that dream carried away by the divided tribes of Babel, the dream of a common language, the dream of language dreaming itself:

> Although translation, unlike art, cannot claim permanence for its products, its goal is undeniably a final, conclusive, decisive stage of all linguistic creation. In translation the original rises into a higher and purer linguistic air. . . . It cannot live there permanently, to be sure; neither can it reach that level in every aspect of the work. Yet in a singularly impressive manner, it at least points the way to this region: the predestined, hitherto inaccessible realm of reconciliation and fulfillment of languages.[12]

For the deconstructionist Paul de Man, embarrassed by Benjamin's meliorist claims for a pure language but sympathetic to the need for a rigorous re-evaluation of the role of translation, the span of difference between poet and translator will once again increase—though now their traditional positions reverse. The translator's role, circumscribed by a linguistic rather than expressive problem, is far less "naive" than the poet's. For unlike the poet—who foolishly believes "that he has to say something, that he has to convey a meaning which does not necessarily relate to language"—the relationship of the translator to the original is "the relationship between language and language, wherein the problem of meaning or the desire to say something, the need to make a statement, is entirely absent."[13] For de Man, the translator remains happily free of the poet's folly of believing that words confer on life an "extra-linguistic meaning." The translator makes, not an approximation of the life *outside* of words, but a proof of the death that was there in language from the outset.

The translator's role in the de Manian plan is both critical and ironic. It calls into question the history of translation and regards it with a deeply suspicious eye. Throughout the ages, the argument goes, translation has served as yet another instrument of "meaning preserving" and hence, one gathers, as yet another player in that field of dreams where language points beyond itself. As one critic soberly explained the flaw behind these dreams: "Determinacy of translation would seem to require determinacy of meaning, for otherwise there fails to be a determinate meaning that is either preserved or lost in translation." [14] Displacing altogether the "lost" object of Frost's old saw, he reduces poetry to a poem's "meaning," then dispenses with them both in one sweep of the hand.

For Rosanna Warren, the relationship between poet and translator is less dichotomous, less hierarchical, and certainly less moribund. The processes of poet and translator, for all their differences in intention, are at some very fundamental level identical to each other— and precisely by the degree of their internal resistance to a declarative or a declarable meaning. As she sees it—having been placed in the curious position of defending the traditionally venerable status of the poet—the "original" process of poetry writing is far less concerned with a fixable meaning than de Man and the deconstructionists would have us believe. As with the translator, the poet comes face to face with that thing which actually distinguishes poetry from other forms of writing—not with its meaning, not with the ideas that happen to form that meaning, not even necessarily with the subject matter from which that meaning tends—but with its requisite, indivisible connection to the *élan vital*, the life force by which language is forged. As Warren goes on to say:

> No one acquainted with literature ever believed in such a chimera as a "meaning" to be preserved apart from its dynamic embodiment in form. . . . It is conventional literary wisdom in the best sense. To take

just one of myriad examples, it is audible in Valéry's statement in his introduction to his translation of Virgil's *Eclogues:* the poet's work "consists less in seeking words for his ideas than in seeking ideas for his words and predominant rhythms." The medium of the literary writer, and especially of the literary translator, was never "meaning" per se but has always been the *linguistic conditions of meaning:* tension, risk, suspicion, the perilous dance of formal language with and away from meaning.[15]

Perhaps one brief example will suffice to show the distinction between "the linguistic conditions of meaning" and "meaning" itself. Consider the closing couplet of Shakespeare's sonnet 73, a meditation on aging and mortality: "This thou perceiv'st, which makes thy love more strong, / To love that well which thou must leave ere long." A reasonable paraphrase of those lines might read: "You have noticed how absence, or the prospect of absence, makes the heart grow fonder." Trivial as that sounds, it fairly approximates the literal meaning of the lines, or at least—interpretive meanings aside—it accurately restates their content. Nonetheless, the paraphrase is wholly inadequate to, and less meaningful than, the original. We have retained a meaning but lost . . . what? Perhaps what Roland Barthes in *The Pleasure of the Text* calls *significance:* "What is significance? It is meaning, *insofar as it is sensually produced.*"[16] And it is sensually produced through what Warren calls its "linguistic conditions": among others, the first strong stress falling with a sudden foreboding on "This"; the dolorous finality of the couplet; the consonantal thematic link between "love" and "leave" and "long"; the measured, dirge-like unfolding of the final monosyllabic line.

Struggle as we will to rephrase Shakespeare's "meaning," the lines exhibit a stubborn resistance to being stated in any way other than the way they are, a self-contained uniqueness that remains a condition of their poetry. It's as though we only get the full meaning of Shakespeare's lines, the meaning plus their significance, by repeating the words exactly as they're written. The meaning has changed from being an *object* excerptable from the words to an *experience* created by the words themselves. What this suggests for poetry translation is a matter of critical importance. For perhaps the higher (if ultimately impossible) task is to carry across, not the meaning or the form—that double bind of traditional translation—but the *significance* of the original. The task is, not to reproduce the content, but with the flint and steel of one's own language to spark what Robert Lowell has called "the fire and finish of the original."

♦

Given the relative freedom with which our age has experimented with literary translation, it seems important to distinguish between a strict translation and a "version," a poem that's somehow modeled on another. A strict translation attempts to reproduce certain identifiable features of the original, its predominant structural, stylistic, and thematic characteristics; and in the economy of that exchange, it attributes "ownership" to the author. A "version," on the other hand, by taking the mantle of authority upon itself, is less bound to those features, and the degree of its divergence determines its independent life, determines the division of ownership between the translator and the poet. This latter category includes adaptations, imitations, interpretations, all literary "mistranslations" of whatever sort.

History has shown that poems of this kind may eventually find a life of their own, independent of the original source. Yeats's "When You Are Old," for example, has virtually erased its connection to Ronsard's "Quand vous serez bien vieille"—the attribution is omitted from both Yeats's *Collected* and *Selected* poems, and the commentaries rarely acknowledge the source. Of course, such renderings can be undertaken with varying motives, with varying degrees of calculation, and with varying claims on the original, so that it's sometimes difficult to say where a "version" ends and a "subversion" or an "aversion" begins.

Feminist translators have taken up this issue of textual authority with a proactive, irreverent, and (at times) willfully controversial boldness. On the assumption that there exists—so the essentialist argument goes—a distinct female language and a distinct male language, it has been proposed that only women should translate women, and only men should translate men. As curious and impractical as that sounds, it poses some interesting questions about the overall project of translation. For example, what are the possibilities, if any, for a relationship between these two languages being established on the translator's ground? Would it be possible for a man to learn the language of women (or vice versa), and, having learned it, would it then be possible to translate from one language into the other? And if these two languages remain, by nature, unavailable to each other, then how are those differences more absolute than the differences between any two languages?

An even more radical feminist position proposes a threefold "corrective" strategy for challenging the rights to textual authority. The most controversial of those strategies, "hijacking," calls for the active appropriation of an "unsympathetic" text and the willful subversion of its intentions. As one practitioner announced in her preface to a "hijacked" text, "My translation practice is a political activity aimed at making language speak for women. So my signature on a translation means: this translation has used every translation strategy to make the feminine visible in language."[17]

The motivations for such "strategies" aren't hard to understand. Imagine the temptations (however unlikely the situation) of a Native American writer translating into Choctaw Robert Frost's poem "The Gift," and in particular the line "The land was ours before we were the land's." It would be hard to resist intervention. But such forays into the land of the other give rise to countervailing problems. For if we license such strategies for an oppressed group, what are we to do when that license falls to the hands of the oppressor (as it inevitably does), an oppressor who, by definition, has broader resources for applying such license? Imagine how one might feel, for example, about a white South African translating into Afrikaans a novel by Toni Morrison and then writing in the preface: "This translation has used every translation strategy to make the white race visible in language."

Suffice it to say, the poet/translator maintains a complex relationship to those rival allegiances, for he or she must mediate between the artistic impulse to take over a text, to overcome its otherness and force its assimilation to one's own language, and that scruple which begs to preserve the integrity of that otherness. Denis Donoghue, in his commentary on the translation into English of an anonymous seventeenth-century love poem in Irish, observes a methodological principle that safeguards the autonomy of the original. For Donoghue, to bend a text too much to one's own sensibility, one's own contemporaneity and language, is to "suppress" whatever "history" the poem contains, the history of its reception and cultural associations. It is to make the "other" less other. This process of internalization which ends in a new poetic product does not, to his mind, sufficiently incorporate a "translator's resistance to his own process," does not sufficiently encourage the original's "recalcitrance," its "principled resistance to the destiny he [the translator] proposed for it." [18] In other words, the translator's duty is not simply to maintain the balance of power between his rendering and the original but to ensure that the original has "retained a mind of its own."

Translations demand to be contextualized, and in a case like the one Donoghue cites—where the resistance addressed is that of an Irish text to an English translation—the concerns reflect more than aesthetic preferences. On the one hand, the suppression of the Irish language under English rule is both literally and symbolically reenacted in that process, a fact no Irish citizen is likely to miss. On the other hand, Donoghue's argument can't be reduced to mere Irish nationalist pride, for the "resistance" he calls for has an added, extrapolitical basis. The whole romantic tradition in European poetry tends to conform to the platonic model of love and *eros* as defined in terms of a union, as realized only when the *two* become *one* (a paradigm we discover implicit in such historical phenomena as colonialism, global marketing, "the new world order," and so on).

But what if our relationship with the other, Donoghue's argument asks, is better as difference than as unity? What if face-to-face is better than fusion? What if the real value of our relationship to the other resides in the impossibility of reducing the other to ourselves, of two subsiding into sameness? In Donoghue's mind, the degree to which a translation obstructs the otherness of the original is the degree to which the other is reduced to oneself, so that the ideal model for translation becomes that which creates the simultaneous experience of both proximity and separateness, intimacy and alterity.

◆

Of course no single form of translation necessarily excludes any other, and perhaps a full understanding of a foreign text necessarily involves a variety of approaches which are constantly renewed in time. As to the question of valuation— of the comparative rewards to be derived from an original and a translation—the criteria are less clear cut, since the only ones qualified to judge are precisely the ones who don't need the translation in the first place. In that sense, the uses of translation might be compared to the adoption of superscripts in opera, outreaching but not excluding the traditional audience of aficionados. Perhaps any discussion of what's satisfying or unsatisfying in a translated text must include the reactions of its "unlanguaged" readers and what they expect from a literary text. For those who need the translation, the value resides not in "accuracy" (which in any case they're unable to judge) but in an access to pleasure, in the manifold aesthetic excitements an independent reading affords.

It is, moreover, a process by which we write language into the future. And by way of illustration, I offer these two observations from Yeats's "The Symbolism of Poetry," observations that, for all their occult curiosity, suggest something of the "afterlife" that any "original" poem begins, and that any translation extends:

> I remember once telling a seeress to ask one among the gods who, as she believed, were standing about her in their symbolic bodies, what would come of a charming but seeming trivial labour of a friend, and the form answering, "the devastation of peoples and the overwhelming of cities."

And:

> I am certainly never sure, when I hear of some war, or of some reli-
> gious excitement or of some new manufacture, or of anything else
> that fills the ear of the world, that it has not all happened because of
> something that a boy piped in Thessaly.[19]

When we think about something being brought into the world that
reverberates into the future, taking forms we could not have foreseen,
we begin to understand the great mystery of literary "belatedness,"
that fateful ongoing echo of the past.

"A translation," as Benjamin put it, "comes later than the original,
and since the important works of world literature never find their
chosen translators at the time of their origin, their translation marks
their stage of continued life."[20] Just as Li Po folded his poems into
paper boats and set them out on the river, so too the translator finds
them tangled in the reeds and sets them out on the current again. For
translation is not only a means by which we come to know the past,
and through the past to know ourselves, it is also the means by which
the future comes to know the past. Through translation the past conspires to engender the future, it seeks without knowing what it seeks,
it anticipates a time that is always other, always unforeseeable, and always to come.

Connoisseurs of Loneliness

James Schuyler and
Elizabeth Bishop

If we think of understatement as lending to words something more than their ordinary meaning—a part of meaning that resides somewhere behind the rhetorical gesture of the words—then James Schuyler and Elizabeth Bishop have made of understatement an overriding aesthetic principle. And though the differing ways each applies that principle is hardly containable by any one example, I'd like to consider the form it takes within the structure of a single poem: "A Few Days" in Schuyler's case, "The End of March" in Bishop's.

What I hope to do is not, however, to interpolate understatement as a "theme" in their poems, but to draw out something of the undermusic, the lyrical sway, which that condition lends to the overall effect of their poems. I would also like to consider their particular uses of understatement as speech acts and, as such, fair representations of their inner lives. For just as Valéry observed that every theory is a carefully prepared fragment of autobiography, so too is every aesthetic preference an expression of the life behind it. In the case of these two poets, that preference is suggestive of a strangely seductive, strangely poignant kind of loneliness—an inwardness, or isolation, or apartness that is, in any case, as cherished as it is suffered, as heartfelt as it is studied, as lyrical and evanescent as it is prosaic and inescapable.

James Schuyler's "A Few Days"

With a distinctly American directness, James Schuyler prefers the literal to the figurative, the well lit to the irradiated, the mundane to the transcendental; and even in his more effusive passages, he shades words into the service of a fluently conversational style. One hears that tendency from the very first words of "A Few Days," a sprawling, diary-like, twenty-eight-page lyric whose title establishes the tone and serves as the poem's opening line:

> are all we have. So count them as they pass. They pass
>   too quickly
> out of breath: don't dwell on the grave, which yawns for
>   one and all.
> Will you be buried in the yard? Sorry, it's against
>   the law.

Schuyler's special blend of the formal and demotic demystifies the one while enlivening the other. The two metaphors in that passage (the out of breath days, the yawning grave) sound so breezily familiar as to be hardly noticeable as metaphors; the fairly regular iambs present themselves in the humdrum of single syllables; and while rhymes crop up all over the place, they are, as in Marianne Moore, uninsistent: the two "pass"s linked glancingly with "breath," the two "all"s directly with "dwell" and "will" but indirectly (and more audibly) with "yawns," "yard," "sorry," and "law." And in the third line, hasn't he casually dropped the most conspicuous of all poetic devices, the literary allusion: the patently American figure of T. S. Eliot's Stetson?

◆

Midway through "A Few Days," in one of countless moments where boredom gives way to a shining, unexpected beatitude, Schuyler releases his attention to what and whatever lies before him. In this case that happens to be:

>   A little
>   trembling worthless
> thing: a mobile. It balances five angels and I lie in bed

> and throw puffs of
> breath at it. It does its shimmering dance.

And so it is that the poet, the sixth angel held in that balance, rises once more out of lethargy into the shimmering dance of consciousness. Consciousness is Schuyler's safe house just as unconsciousness is his house of cards, and most of the myriad, freehand sketches that compose this poem will come into being at the very moment when dullness seems most threatening. In a refreshing reversal of the traditional pose, the poet seems less *stimulated* than *bored* into verse, the yawning void only held at bay by an act of willed inspiration: a puff of breath thrown in the direction of some "little trembling worthless thing."

That initial state of glittering awareness typically becomes the jumping-off point for spontaneous musings:

> It rained earlier today: I
> lay on the bed
> and watched the beads it formed on the foliage of
> my balcony balustrade
> drop of their own weight. I remember the night the
> house in Maine
> was struck by lightning. . . .

Schuyler's poems are a kind of whistling in the dark, and I suspect that part of their garrulousness has something to do with his feeling that poetry, while an inadequate substitute for life itself ("I / have always been / more interested in truth than in imagination"), becomes a useful stand-in when life withdraws. He appears to share Yeats's sentiment that "friendship is all the house I have," and when "there is no one to talk / to, nothing to talk / about," then poetry, like his beloved radio ("that anodyne of the lonely"), fills the silence of those empty rooms. In the absence of others, the poet turns to *soliloquia*, to his own unique version of "dialogues with myself."

As with most of our private conversations, Schuyler calls down, through a welter of memory and free association, those disembodied spirits "whose footsteps over our hearts," as Yeats observed, "we call emotion." Flowers, sex, snippets of gossip, past and present loves, bowel movements, paintings, lunches and cologne, "the dream shop and the dram shop" of reverie: all engage him equally when he's passing the time alone. That he doesn't worry about having "something to say"—or even too much about the artistic mediocrity which shadows the random—gives his work both the feel and clutter of a diary.

It may go without saying that Schuyler's pronounced indifference to conventional strategies for making poems is, improbably, part of his charm. (No doubt it is also what keeps some readers, disoriented without those conventions, from experiencing his weirdly personal brand of joie de vivre: Schuyler can get enthused about buying "striped socks from a barrow.") For all forward-looking poets, accepted "ways of making" are the art's Bastille and words the crowds they gather at the gates. But the authority of Schuyler's protest—playful and unreformist as it is—derives from those age-old powers of enchantment by which, according to Roland Barthes, even diaries can achieve the frisson we associate with literature: "the individuation, the scent, the seduction, the fetishism of language" (*The Pleasure of the Text*). More simply, in a collage of seemingly genial, offbeat, free-form improvisations, this self-styled rhapsode of the "worthless thing" takes his case directly to the senses, to that prospect where poetry launches its stones.

◆

In addition to Schuyler's melange of friends, lovers, family, and acquaintances, an assortment of chance characters appear in this poem as well. They are an unlikely yet telling group, and his quickness to respond, if only to the looming distance between them, awakens a rueful compassion that is a hallmark of his poems:

> On the train across the aisle
> from me there was a young couple.
> He read while she stroked the flank of his chest in a
> circular motion, motherly,

covetous. They kissed. What is lovelier than young love?
>   Will it only lead
to barren years of a sour marriage? They were perfect
>   together. I wish
them well.

As this passage suggests, Schuyler's romanticism contains its own built-in curb, for again like Yeats he seems highly conscious of the toll time takes. As in "Among School Children," where Yeats imagines a room of students "with sixty or more winters" on their heads, Schuyler almost reflexively projects old age onto the young. Or, in equally heavy-hearted ways, he extrapolates a youth from the old and defeated: when he sees a man lying on the street, "one shoe off, his shirt un- / buttoned down to his / navel," he thinks, "Poor guy: once he was / a little boy." Perhaps not until the end of the poem do we fully understand—so effectively does Schuyler submerge such things as "themes" and "subjects"—that closeted within this solicitude, indeed within the very distractedness of the narration itself, lies the approaching death of the poet's mother.

She has appeared before in Schuyler's work (most notably in "The Morning of the Poem"), and, as Howard Moss has pointed out, over time she became "a character of strength and integrity, assuming a role somewhat akin to Proust's grandmother, the central moral figure of *À la recherche du temps perdu*." When we first encounter her in "A Few Days," she is "almost eighty-nine," "her sight is failing," and when he goes to visit her in his brother's house, she says, "I can't see you but I know your / voice!" For the rest of the poem her presence is more felt than drawn—she appears only twice more, briefly, before the final pages—though framing the poem as she does, her shadow falls over each of its pages. From the very beginning, we can sense Schuyler mediating between the world outside and a foreboding within:

A pretty blond child sat next to me for a while. She
>   had a winning smile,
but I couldn't talk to her, beyond "What happened to
>   your shoes?" "I put them under the seat." And

so she had. She pressed the button that released the
    seat back and sank
back like an old woman.

At this point a reader only vaguely realizes that Schuyler's journey has
something to do with death. And that winsome little girl who appears to have stepped from a Salinger story seems another diversion
in the "eight hours / of boredom on the train." But, as we eventually
discover, her unexpected fall into old age painfully prefigures, twenty-
seven pages later, the last lines of the poem:

Margaret Daisy Connor Schuyler Ridenour,
rest well,
the weary journey done.
    ◆

"A few days: how to celebrate them?" The opposing terms of that
sentence—portentous on the one hand, cheerful on the other—re-
hearse a dialogue that Schuyler often has with himself. The first half
of the sentence poses a wistful riddle on mortality; the second half
responds with the poet's charge: how to make the best of our fleeting
and dolorous lives. While the poem's occasion (if his mother's death
can be called that) would lead most poets to censor all but the most
austere details, Schuyler turns his warm, unembellishing light on the
inchoate clutter of our daily world. The following, which contains
one of two appearances his mother makes before the closing pages,
exemplifies both his predicament and his method:

    It's today I want
to memorialize but how can I? What is there to it?
    Cold coffee and
a ham-salad sandwich? A skinny peach tree holds no
    peaches. Molly howls
at the children who come to the door. What did they
    want? It's the wrong
time of year for Girl Scout cookies.
My mother can't find her hair net. She nurses a cup of
    coffee substitute, since

her religion (Christian Science) forbids the use
　　of stimulants. On this
desk, a vase of dried blue flowers, a vase of artificial
　　roses, a bottle with
a dog for stopper, a lamp, two plush lions that hug
　　affectionately, a bright
red travel clock, a Remington Rand, my Olivetti, the
　　ashtray and the coffee cup.

For some readers, such random, uninflected lists will no doubt
prove a chore—compared, for example, to the consciously orchestrated lists in Whitman or Hopkins or Wordsworth—and perhaps
they are. But as much as we feel a perfunctory democracy in the busyness of such lines, we also feel a special emphasis that would surely
disappear in the face of more mannered attentions. The bric-a-brac
on that desk provides for Schuyler what "white hawthorn," "pastoral
eglantine," and "the coming musk rose" provided for Keats. As Stevens has remarked of his own imagination, Schuyler's light adds nothing to the world except itself. And yet *what* that light illuminates figures as part of its drama. In an effect resembling scumbling, he softens
those hard, hieratic edges by which we classify, value, rank, divide, so
that the agreeable and unsavory, the profound and the fatuous, the
excruciatingly personal and the world's news, all converge on the neutral ground of the poem's page.

　　"Are secrets a / way of telling lies?" he asks himself, as if selectiv-
ity were another way of keeping secrets. "Yes, they are." And while
not keeping secrets is no guarantee of telling the truth, it may at least
help tell fewer untruths. If one may talk about moral inclinations in
Schuyler's work, that is one. Another is his resolve to make us look
again, through his own freely tendered affections, at the overlooked
and unlovely. The snowdrop in a poem by that same title is an example of this:

(Reginald
Farrer hated snowdrops: in his

Yorkshire rock garden the rain
beat them down into the mud
and they got all dirty. Why not
pick a few, wash them off and
make a nosegay in a wineglass,
Reginald?)

Such unadvertised restorations remind us that poetry has often taken
as its proper subject the truly negligible things of this world. And to
pluck them from the dirt of our neglect, to dust them off and represent them to us in a wineglass has always been one of its functions.
It may be that inconsequence is the hallmark of Schuyler's poems, but
by accepting, indeed by paying homage to that condition which (let's
face it) composes the larger part of our lives, he brings us closer to
the wondrous, irretrievable here and now:

Tomorrow is another day, but no better than today if
    you only realize it.
Let's love today, the what we have now, this day, not
    today or tomorrow or
yesterday, but this passing moment, that will
    not come again.

Elizabeth Bishop's "The End of March"

On the dust jacket of Elizabeth Bishop's *Complete Poems*, Robert Lowell observes that "When we read her, we enter the classical serenity
of a new country." If we hear our own doubts in that description
(ours is an age not easily characterized by the classical or the serene),
then we also hear the hope which is the treatment for our convention. If we enter a new country when we read her, then a new country enters us as well; and it's the emotional color, the topographical
feel of that country that I'd like to investigate here.

To do that requires a few prefactory observations. Of all the poets of her generation, Bishop most nearly approaches (hence most
nearly retrieves) the idea and the ideal of the perfectible poem. In a

sonnet from *History*, Lowell hints at the extraordinary restraint which made that possible:

> ... *Do*
> you still hang your words in air, ten years unfinished,
> glued to your notice board, with gaps or empties for the
> unimaginable phrase—unerring Muse who makes the casual per-
> fect? ("Calling 1970")

Given the demands of her "unerring Muse," it comes as no surprise that Bishop produced such a remarkably small number of poems. Over a writing life which spanned nearly forty-five years, she published fewer than ninety poems, and that reserve carried over into her private life as well. She avoided, for the most part, public readings and interviews; she dissociated herself from "schools" and literary movements; and she served only a few short stints teaching in colleges and universities.

If it didn't suggest something anachronistic, one could say that there's a touch of the eremite about her. She can be painfully reclusive, yet she can also evoke a disarmingly intimate (if decidedly disembodied) sense of herself through her poems. And like someone "all alone above an extinct world" ("Objects and Apparitions"), she regards the world with that curious pathos which burnishes what is passing away. Her now-famous method, which Marianne Moore called "enumerative description," remains the most celebrated aspect of her work, and I won't pretend to add to that discussion. What I'd like to do instead is focus on a quality without which that method could quickly become, in less mindful hands, patchy, earth-bound, aleatory, or jejune.

The quality I refer to is *patience*, a patience born of the realization that, in the world of appearances, reality lasts only "as long as this phrase lasts" ("Objects and Apparitions"). Moreover, in Bishop's case, it seems reality lasts only as long as one willingly accepts that heightened solitude which the deepest forms of attention require.

For one can only truly be patient when one recognizes that, beyond the door, no one is waiting for that patience to end.

This quality becomes all the more radical when we remember that Bishop arrived at a time when the ruling orthodoxies in poetry were urging a very different approach. To take one prominent example, Ezra Pound's Imagist dictum was simple and unequivocal—*condensare*—condense, compact, concentrate, trim. A principle of physics establishes that when matter is compressed it becomes more volatile, and a similar principle governs Pound's theory of the image. Subjected to a process of intense concentration, the particular acquires a heightened energy which Pound called *luminosity*. In terms of time, that concentration occurs by contracting, or foreshortening, the act of perception, by snaring one's subject on the wing: the emotional complex caught in an *instant* of time. And regardless of what poets have felt about Imagism since, that single principle of composition has held great sway over this century.

But then, one might say, along came Elizabeth Bishop, and along came poems like "The Map," "A Cold Spring," "The Bight," "At the Fishhouses," "Questions of Travel," and "Under the Window: Ouro Prêto." And something very different started happening. The method, it seemed, was in the *waiting*, in allowing the eye to *linger*, in the feeling that the imagination—like the grandparents' voices in "The Moose"—can *take its time* "uninterruptedly / talking, in Eternity." It was a new cognitive music, a new way of hearing the mind, and it was a music inseparable from the poem's ostensible subject. The poet's intuitive responses to the world became, not the uniquely entitled subject of the poet, but another set of things within that world. Bishop's poems remind us that attention, that faculty which Simone Weil called "the very substance of prayer," is another name for the imagination.

That reminder awakens a feeling for those everyday wonders which attention frees from the chain of fact, a feeling with roots in what Emerson called "the joy of the beholding and jubilant soul."

And that persistent transaction between object, eye and mind becomes an ultimate dramatic concern, a theater within which the mind plays out the siren-call "to see what it was I saw." This makes a reader feel awfully lucky to be hanging around when Bishop is doing pretty ordinary things, as she is in "The End of March," one of what I'm inclined to call "the late masterpieces" from *Geography III.*

The poem recounts a walk the poet takes ("in rubber boots" no less) along the seashore in Duxbury. This is one of the rare poems in which Bishop actually appears as a "character" (though that may overstate the case), but it's also revealing in another way, for it points up the poet's disinclination to hasten the poem to its end. Consider this: a man is hurrying down the street to mail a letter, but in order to remember what he wrote in the letter, he slows his pace, as if that slower tread were somehow essential to remembering. It's that same sense of a necessary slowness one feels when, mid-poem, Bishop pauses to refine her first perception, or to ask herself a question, or to issue a private aside:

>   . . . that crooked box
> set up on pilings, shingled green,
> a sort of artichoke of a house, but greener
> (boiled with bicarbonate of soda?),
> protected from spring tides by a palisade
> of—are they railroad ties?
> (Many things about this place are dubious.)
> I'd like to retire there and do *nothing,*
> or nothing much, forever, in two bare rooms:
> look through binoculars, read boring books,
> old, long, long books, and write down useless notes. . . .

By exposing, as she does, the inner workings of the poem—like the magician who, while performing his illusions, keeps telling the audience how the illusions are made—Bishop confers on her readers the impression (or the fact?) that if we paid attention we might see the same things she did, and see them in the very same way.

In that context, I'd like to look at one of the least eventful and most understated passages in the poem:

> On the way back our faces froze on the other side.
> The sun came out for just a minute.
> For just a minute, set in their bezels of sand,
> the drab, damp, scattered stones
> were multi-colored,
> and all those high enough threw out long shadows,
> individual shadows, then pulled them in again.

John Hollander has referred to the "almost infernal particularity" of these lines, though it's a somewhat different music I hear, a music more finely attuned to her characteristic instinct for self-effacement. One notices how refined an instinct that is in the ease with which the "poet" is eclipsed, not only by appearing to take so little credit for her discoveries—what are they, she seems to say, but mental notes of a type that memory ordinarily keeps?—but also, and more importantly, by refusing to make the image appear more "magical" than it actually is. A poet more conscious of modernist codes might've condensed this to a quatrain:

> Set in their bezels of sand,
> the multi-colored stones
> threw out long shadows
> then pulled them in again.

However inferior this version may be, its image appears more "poetic"—or, to use Pound's term, more "luminous"—more the construction of a specialized sensibility. In any case, it clearly appears more "made." To that degree, the poet's presence is accentuated, the poet's facility (no mere mental notation) occupies a larger space on the stage. Like the magician pretending to his supernatural powers, the poet becomes the imaginative source—and the conjurer's gift, not the collapsible hat, receives our rapt applause.

In Bishop's version—as though the hat were acknowledged as the source all along—we're included in the process by which the image appears in the world. And the accumulation of fairly run-of-the-mill adjectives—"drab," "damp," "scattered," "multi-colored," "long," "individual"—only further serve to make the poem a less rarefied utterance, less the fancy of the Poet than a careful gathering of perceptions drawn from daily life.

In one very fundamental sense, Bishop has managed, and managed by example, to demystify the role of the poet. Ruskin saw this as the highest calling of the artist, perhaps even of humankind; as he wrote in *Modern Painters* (in a passage, by the way, which Marianne Moore recorded in her notebooks), "The greatest thing a human soul ever does in this world is to see something, and tell what it saw in a plain way. Hundreds of people can talk for one who can think, but thousands can think for one who can see." [1]

Of course, Bishop's method should not be confused with the artless or the accidental; nor should it be construed as yet another form of twentieth-century nihilism. Howard Moss, one of Bishop's early and lifelong admirers, has written revealingly about the sophisticated operations, and the secret ethos, of her deceptively simple style: "We test an image by its reality, and by its reality we test the truthfulness of the writer. It is by what one chooses to see and *how* one chooses to see it that this underground proving takes place. Not only does the image lead us to comparisons and therefore to thought, but those eyes, in a second, put both the viewed and the viewer onto the scale."

Kafka was said to have tacked a piece of paper above his writing table, and on that paper was written the single word *Warten*—"Wait." To read Bishop's poems is to learn, among other things, the far-reaching aesthetic and ethical implications of that profoundly difficult lesson. It is also to learn to attend more fully to the vast resource of our inner lives, to what the child narrator of Bishop's story "The Village" calls our "immense, sibilant, glistening loneliness."

A Solving Emptiness

C. K. Williams and
Charles Wright

Keeping in mind certain ideas ventured earlier in these pages, I want to turn from more or less speculative to more or less practical matters. The opportunity for this detour arrives by way of two editors who asked me independently to review a book of poems. One of those books was C. K. Williams's *Flesh and Blood,* the other was Charles Wright's *Zone Journals;* and early on in the note-taking stage, as I was finding my way from poem to poem, a series of somewhat tangential issues presented themselves to me. For these two collections, so different in kind, ambition, and sensibility, shared a surprising number of traits: Each was written mid-career, each established a new orientation to the earlier work, each sought freshened energy through a dramatic dilation of the line, and each was buoyed by a tide of newly inclusive materials. As if to prove there is, after all, a second act in American lives, these books served as testaments of faith, the kind of faith that seems to surface from the crisis of our middle years, from that dawning awareness of a "solving emptiness," as Philip Larkin put it, "that lies just under all we do."

If despair was the instigation for these changes, then a renewed confidence in the restorative properties of poetry would prove to be the response. Their shared subject was authority, perseverance, the triumph of the imagination over the leveling forces of time. Heartening as all that was (and they're both very heartening books), the depth of their determination alerts one to the depth of an underlying fear and I soon found myself wondering less about the milestone each book marked and more about the shuntings, detours, and misdirections by which each poet had come to form, in the mirror of his work, some lasting idea of who he is. One thing was certain: they hadn't come to it easily.

C. K. Williams's *Flesh and Blood*

The journey that ended in *Flesh and Blood* may have been the more fitful of the two, if only because, from the perspective of the earlier books, it's the least foreseeable. After two decades of wrestling by turns with discursive and dramatic modes, Williams found a form supple enough to accommodate both those tendencies. Each of its 147 eight-line poems is set in a highly alliterative, double pentameter line—normally ten strong stresses played across an unpredictable number of syllables—that recalls Old English or Hopkins's sprung rhythm. To anchor that line, and to save it from bombast, Williams employs a gritty, street-wise realism, a manner that assumes the charged vernacular of the "common man." The play of the colloquial against the rung-out carillons of that long line gives his poems uncanny tonal range, mimetic of thought reeling in flux between the worlds of experience and contemplation.

It may be that Williams has accomplished for the long line what William Carlos Williams did for the short one: he has re-cast it in a way that a reader discovers some new activity of the mind, some fresh correlation of eye and ear, heart and intellect, as though the mundane world were suddenly infused with a newly-awakened energy. More often than not, the experience of these poems is like a ride on a roller coaster: Once you get on, you don't get off, and the thrill comes from the slow, tantalizing rise to a height from which you pitch down in a blinding swirl of syntactic reversals, rhythmic shifts, dialectical turns:

> They're at that stage where so much desire streams
> between them, so much frank need and want,
> so much absorption in the other and the self and the
> self-admiring entity and unity they make—

> her mouth so full, breast so lifted, head thrown back
>   *so* far in her laughter at his laughter,
> he so solid, planted, oaky, firm, so resonantly factual
>   in the headiness of being craved so,
> she almost wreathed upon him as they intertwine. . . .
> that just to watch them is to feel again that hitching
>   in the groin, that filling of the heart,
> the old, sore heart, the battered, foundered, faithful
>   heart, snorting again, stamping in its stall. ("Love: Beginnings")

The breathless insistence of Williams's line gives ordinary moments a stupefying psychological power, an Orphic music. With a microscopic eye that notch by notch closes in on its subject, he magnifies the book's innumerable vignettes through a mass of adjectives, adverbs, and nouns, through the line's own headlong, downhill pace, through the studied uses of repetition ("so much . . . so much . . . so much," she "so full . . . so lifted . . . so far," etc.). And like a photographic blow-up, this magnification tests reality's surfaces—"he so solid, planted, oaky, firm," "she almost wreathed upon him as they intertwine"—until it finally yields what lies beneath: in this case, a heady mix of vanity and sex.

Interestingly enough, since Williams's poems have always exhibited a nagging social conscience, it's not in the arena of human behavior but in that underworld of motive and impulse that his poetry reaches critical mass: "just to watch them is to feel again that hitching in the groin, that filling of the heart, / the old, sore heart, the battered, foundered, faithful heart, snorting again, stamping in its stall." This poem contains all the signature elements of Williams's later style: the extended, refracted line; the perceptive sense tuned like an aerial to the daily round; the explicit gloss on some commonplace scene; the universal story suddenly revealed underpinning the individual moment.

But how did he arrive at that style, one asks? On the evidence of the earlier work, one can only imagine that it must have entailed a torturous period of self-examination, a period of rethinking the very basis of his art. For while the same thematic preoccupations haunt Williams's work from the beginning, in the first two books—*Lies* (1969) and *I Am the Bitter Name* (1972)—those leaps to significance, couched as they are in a style ill-suited to discourse or analysis, rarely sound like anything more than didactic dreams.

Although those books now read like juvenilia, they're worth revisiting if only to gauge the magnitude of the change they preceded. The following, spoken by a garrulous, if fiendish, trash collector, typifies the earlier style:

> What do they do with kidneys and toes
> in hospitals? And where did your old dog go
> who peed on the rug and growled?
> They are at my house now, and what grinds
> in your wife's teeth while she sleeps
> is mine. She is chewing
> on embryos, on the eyes of your lover. . . .
> And in your body,
> the one who died there and rots
> secretly in the fingers of your spirit,
> she is hauling his genitals out, basket
> after basket
> and mangling all of it in the crusher. ("Trash")

We may infer from details that the "you" is male, probably a suburban middle-class American (that arch-villain of the 1960s), whose inner life "rots / secretly" and whose inadequacies and apparent infidelities have transformed his wife, if only in her dreams, into a monstrous, cannibalistic machine. Pitted against them, the trash collector serves as the nightmare voice of the subconscious world. But something childish, something even cartoonlike and silly negates the squalor of this grisly scene. The details feel almost flagrantly excessive (especially the "basket / after basket" of "his genitals"—wouldn't the normal measure of his anatomy be enough?), and since we never really learn why this man has sunk to such depravities, we can't help wonder: Is it truly as bad as all that?

To be fair, I suppose we're being urged to trust that the speaker's nausea symptomatically registers a disgust with his time and place, though here too we're never given particulars: America's war in Viet Nam? Mississippi's vicious repression of voter registration drives? Los Angeles's police action in Watts? Since Williams rarely ventured beyond generalities in those days, we're left with a series of *actes gratuits* and with surprisingly bloodless stabs at significance.

Williams has acknowledged his early debt to Vallejo, Neruda, and Miguel Hernández, but more than any stylistic traits or political affinities what appears to have crossed over into his work is the picturesque—a quixotic, impassioned ardor that often leads to the excesses we see above. But young poets soon learn from their foreign influences that the atmospherics of another country resist transplanting to one's native soil; and with Williams's third book, he appears to fall under a different and more compatible influence: Walt Whitman.

Certainly we feel the presence of Whitman's ropy lines, his abundance and swagger, his hearty erotics and self-satisfactions, his profound rootedness in what he called "the large unconscious scenery of my land." The impact of Whitman's presence is remarkable:

> The men working on the building going up here have got
>   these great,
> little motorized wheelbarrows that're supposed to be for lugging
>   bricks and mortar
> but that they seem to spend most of their time barrel-assing up
>   the street in,
> racing each other or trying to con the local secretaries into
>   taking rides in the bucket. ("The Sanctity")

In place of the studied mannerisms of the previous two books, Williams adopts a blithely natural tone. We hear it in the way the lines mimic the jaunty colloquialisms—"that're," "barrel-assing," "con," and "guys"—of the construction workers; the way the preposition suspended until the end of line three is grammatically awkward yet conversationally true; the way the sentence unfolds in the raucous cadences of a tavern bard. That workaday strain of American speech will play across every line that Williams writes in the years to come. From a lachrymose New-World Job venting his sufferings in the language of abuse to this deft, street-talking populist—that's a pretty thorough self-revision, and one can't help but wonder what prompted it.

During this period, Williams was working on the translation (with Gregory W. Dickerson) of Sophocles's *Women of Trachis.* It seems possible that, in coming to terms with the formal demands of the play, he felt the allure of narrative, for he abandons his earlier surrealist stance and starts fashioning poems as vehicles for storytelling and rumination. Because narrative is more accessible to the everyday reader, something in Williams's proletarian leanings must've felt more at home in its structures; moreover, it provided a context in which to ground his habitual speculative side.

Accordingly, in the next three books Williams turns for his materials to the actual and historic, all the while abjuring the mystifications—or at least the more ornate embellishments—of poetry. He now asks that his poems be judged not by some abstract idea of poetic ingenuity but by the urgency with which they're wrested from life. The following passage from "Spit" recounts the story of a Nazi who begins to spit into a Rabbi's mouth *"so that the Rabbi could continue to spit on the Torah"*:

> All these ways to live that have something to do with how
> > we live
> and that we're almost ashamed to use as metaphors for
> > what goes on in us
> but that we do anyway . . .
> > > and God is what it is when
> > we're alone
> wrestling with solitude and everything speaking in our
> > souls turns against us like His fury
> and just facing another person, there is so much terror
> > and hatred that yes,
> spitting in someone's mouth, trying to make him defile

his own meaning,
 would signify the struggle to survive each other and what
   we'll enact to accomplish it.

That Williams sees this moment, not as an isolated act of individual cruelty, but as one of those "ways we live that have something to do with how we live," points to a deepening consciousness in his work. His interest in the link between the behavioral and psychological has been mirrored all along in his discrete uses of figurative and discursive language. But this new sanction to speak about abstract things in abstract terms calls up an old quandary which form itself cannot resolve: how to make a poem that unites the worlds of plot and rumination while still maintaining the linear insistence of poetry.

Until now Williams worked in the two modes separately; in *Tar*, he begins to weave them together. And given the huge demands of that ambition, it's no surprise that the book's true muse derives less from poetry than the novel. "I think it's probably been Dostoevski more than anyone else," he remarked in an interview from that period, "who's been the deep novelistic influence. I've always been in great awe of him, of his inexhaustible moral energy . . . the way he is always in touch with the larger questions." It's easy to see what in Dostoevski so attracted Williams's interest. Like the Underground Man, who declares "that to be conscious is an illness—a real thoroughgoing illness," Williams sets out to dramatize "the malleable, / mazy, convoluted matter of the psyche" and to set it in opposition to a brutish world.

For all the satisfactions that must have come with *Tar*, Williams continued to push for a poem of both immediacy and elaboration. While *Tar* returns like memory to revise and make sense of the past, *Flesh and Blood* proves an unblinking eye that convenes the disorderly present:

The way she tells it, they were in the Alps or somewhere, tall, snow-
    capped mountains anyway,
 in their hotel, a really nice hotel, she says, they'd decided that for

once they'd splurge.
They'd just arrived, they were looking from their terrace out across
    a lake or bay or something.
She was sitting there, just sitting there and thinking to herself how
    pleasant it all looked,
like a postcard, just the way for once it's supposed to look, clean
    and pure and cool,
when his hand came to her shoulder and he asked her something,
    "Don't you think it's lovely?"
then something else, his tone was horrid; there was something that he
    wanted her to say—
how was *she* to know what he wanted her to say?—and he *shook* her
    then, until she ached. ("The Marriage")

I quote this poem in its entirety to demonstrate the manner by which Williams scales down his narratives. In the first clause, he quickly fixes the event: a story the married woman has confided to the narrator and the narrator in turn confides to the reader. Next, he filters her story through the narrator's consciousness, which distills the most resonant features. Novelistic particulars, the "Alps or somewhere" and "a lake or bay or something," are muted in favor of essences, "the way for once it's supposed to look, clean and pure and cool." Like a portraitist blurring background detail to more carefully focus the subject, Williams obscures everything around the troubled wife. In the end, that scrutiny turns to identification, and in the final three lines the narrator's voices merges with hers in the rising craziness of the moment: "how was *she* to know what he wanted her to say?—and he *shook* her then, until she ached."

The vicissitudes of a restless, headstrong mind are Williams's trademark, but the evolution of his work is more aptly characterized by the thresholds in his development: from the early, self-absorbed, self-dramatizing poet, to the outward-looking Dostoevskian narrator, to the immediate, unblinking, spectral witness of *Flesh and Blood*. That one generally feels equal to his poems (and part of their appeal *is* their accessibility) we must attribute to Williams's determination to find a style that, while blending the dramatic and discursive, bluntly refuses to refine the human figure out of its unkempt, shaggy form.

Charles Wright's *Zone Journals*

By his own accounting, Charles Wright's seventh book of poems, *Zone Journals*, brings to a close the middle phase—and launches the beginning of the final phase—of his prolific career. But this, it turns out, reveals much more than the structural plan of his life's work; for in the closing circle that plan describes, Wright marks out the same imperishable pattern Eliot traced in the ash of "Little Gidding": "What we call the beginning is often the end / And to make an end is to make a beginning"; and "the end of all our exploring / Will be to arrive where we started / And know the place for the first time." Given the nature of such arrivals, the heartfelt, home-going pathos of *Zone Journals* is heightened by a chronological reading of Wright's work, a reading which charts the slow but certain process by which that pattern has come to fix itself in the mind's eye of this poet.

Wright's first four books, republished in 1982 as *Country Music,* comprise the first phase in his project; the next three, concluding with *Zone Journals,* comprise the second, collected under the title *The World of the 10,000 Things.* Looking back over those books, one discovers that Wright has cultivated a certain set of concerns, that he's been writing about them from the beginning, and, one suspects, he'll keep writing about them to the end; and that those same concerns have served, in turn, as the chemical solution into which he's dipped the negative of his grand design. If any one passage could suggest those concerns, this might do:

> —Ficino tells us the Absolute
> Wakens the drowsy, lights the obscure,
>
> revives the dead,
> Gives form to the formless and finishes the incomplete.
> What better good can be spoken of? ("A Journal of the Year of the
> Ox," 9 May 1985)

To waken, illuminate, revive, give form, and finally to complete—it would be difficult to find other activities of equal value in Wright's poems. It would also be difficult to find another contemporary as willing to trace those energies back to the notion of an Absolute (though it's important to note that—instead of "What better good can be *done*" —Wright says "What better good can be *spoken of,*" thereby suspending the question of faith). That he has managed to build a career around those calculated uncertainties—in a day and age when such things arouse more skepticism than interest—attests to the solitariness of his enterprise and to the sheer verbal power of the poems.

As is evident now, Wright is a poet of projects and paradoxes, large, ambitious, ongoing projects paradoxically enfleshed in an art that moves—"line after line after latched, untraceable line" ("A Journal of English Days")—less by will than intuition. Like some huge Gothic stained glass window, his books coalesce into elaborately patterned fragments of perception whose splendor depends on the brilliance of the verbally projected light with which he suffuses their pages. Light, in fact, may be the single most instructive element in his poems, the only element to cross with ease between this world and the next (his twinned perennial subjects), and it comprises the medium from which *Zone Journals* derives its abiding principle of composition: "the more luminous anything is, / The more it subtracts what's around it, . . . / making the unseen seen" ("Yard Journal").

At this point in his career, Wright seems called to test both the verse and converse of that axiom. Is it also true that the more one subtracts the more luminous the thing becomes? Somewhere within those precepts resides the imagist's and visionary's paradigm, although (again paradoxically) Wright's shrewdly subtractive style is never more expansive than in *Zone Journals*. In the course of its packed ninety-eight pages, stories get told; kin of the spirit and kin of the flesh appear, speak, leave their names; dates are recorded religiously ("October 17, Sir Philip [Sidney] dead / 397 years today"); and ideas spool out *almost* to the point of assertion.

As Wright described his method in a *Paris Review* interview, the ten "journals" that make up this collection inhabit "as loose a form as I can work with and still work in lines" (making them the orchestral counterpart of *China Trace*, which, ten years earlier, in another interview, he declared "was as tight as I could get it"). "One of the purposes of the journals," he goes on to say, "was to work with a line that was pushed as hard as I could push it toward prose. . . . At the same time, of course, they *are* poems, with all a poem's avoidances and exclusions. Still the word 'journal' is operative, and allows more quotidiana in." [1]

If the word "journal" best serves to describe the feel of the poems, then "exclusion" best serves to describe how they work ("Exclusion's the secret," one poem confides). With sudden cross-cuts into discourse, narrative, dreamscape, flashback, and interior monologue, the journals set up relations which, mutually stirred, resolve in time into a sustained investigation of his favorite themes: "the difference between the spirit and flesh" ("A Journal of English Days"), "the inarticulation of desire" ("Light Journal"), "the presence / Of what is missing" ("Chinese Journal"), and, ever present, the feel of how it feels to be "Lashed to the syllable and noun, / the strict Armageddon of the verb" ("A Journal of True Confessions").

Our epoch and Wright's cosmology would stifle a less determined poet, but even when reality proves most unyielding, most resistant to his vexed metaphysical probings—as in the following section from "A Journal of the Year of the Ox"—resistance itself is anatomized and subsumed into the articulated music of his inner life:

These monochromatic early days of October
Throb like a headache just back of the eyes,

                                         a music
Of dull, identical syllables
Almost all vowels,

                    ooohing and aaahing
As though they would break out in speech and tell us something.

But nothing's to be revealed,

It seems:
> each day the shadows blur and enlarge,
> the rain comes and comes back,
A dripping of consonants,
As though it too wanted to tell us something, something
Unlike the shadows and their stray signs,

Unlike the syllable the days make
Behind the eyes, cross-current and cross-grained, and unlike
The sibilance of oak tree and ash. (4 October 1985)

Wright appears to have more in common with the early modernists than with anyone in his day. Much has already been said about Pound's influence—so much so that the label seems to have stuck long past the point Wright outgrew it—and something still remains to be said about Eliot's. Wright's particular brand of classicism, for example, with its carefully mediated forays on the tradition, derives more from Eliot's connoisseurism than from Pound's vortex. But given his extraordinary ability to question the things he values most —not to mention his lavish iconographic imagination and his residual faith in the efficacy of certain personal signs—he reminds me more of Yeats, the one modernist with whom, so far as I know, he has yet to be compared.

In my opinion, it is one of Wright's most significant accomplishments that, like Yeats, he has managed to maintain as the basis of his faith a dogged, indefatigable doubt. Upon the echoing hollowness of his place in time, he has constructed a dialogue of self and soul that's both credible and unapologetic at once. And though little of Yeats's music finds its way into Wright's line, many of his predilections do. The following, for example, from Yeats's *Ideas of Good and Evil*, not only applies to Wright's kaleidoscopic style but anticipates one of the metaphysical issues that haunts *Zone Journals* throughout: the summoning of presences from the "other world": "All sounds, all colours, all forms . . . call down among us certain disembodied powers, whose footsteps over our hearts we call emotions; . . . and the more perfect [the work of art] is, and the more various and numerous the elements that have flowed into its perfection, the more powerful will be the emotion, the power, the god it calls among us."[2]

The "disembodied powers" Wright calls down among us—powers no less various than St. Catherine, Jefferson, Li Po, Dante, the Cherokee nation, Buddha, Dickinson, Leonardo, Poe, just to name a few—those powers become, as he says in "A Journal of the Year of the Ox," his "constituency":

> those who would die back
> To splendor and rise again
> From hurt and unwillingness,
> their own ash on their tongues,
> Are those I would be among,
> The called, the bruised by God, by their old ways forsaken
> And startled on. (12 October 1985)

And their footsteps over those pages account in part for the slowly developing object of Wright's quest. This is not spiritual archaeology so much as portraiture by collage; and the portrait, we have come to see, is of Him "whose face," as St. Augustine described it, "is ever to be sought."

The completion of this stage in Wright's "project" invites some speculative comment. Perhaps because of the perilous terrain these poems have crossed—Banquo's ghost would have felt right at home—one grows more aware of the conscious elegance of their lines, their keen refinements, the kind of sangfroid that, unfaltering, says: This poet never loses his cool. And yet, when one turns back to those saints, visionaries, mad seers, and mystics who people Wright's poems, one can't help recall that their journeys into "the other world" cost nothing less than apostasy and terror. It wasn't just symmetry, but a fearful symmetry that Blake discovered, a blood-dimmed tide that Yeats foresaw.

That Wright has achieved such a profound level of virtuosity is as ominous as it is admirable, for virtuosity now becomes the obstacle.

In a bittersweet section from "A Journal of the Year of the Ox," the poet is relaxing outside his home, "The quattrocento landscape / turning to air beneath [his] feet," children in the distance playing "a game [he'd] never played," his son and friend moving "through the upper yard like candles / Among the fruit trees." In the sustained evanescence of that wistful hour the poet suspects "That anything I could feel / anything I could put my hand on"

> Would burst into brilliance at my touch.
> But I sat still, and I touched nothing,
>   afraid that something might change
> And change me beyond my knowing,
> That everything I had hoped for, all I had ever wanted,
> Might actually happen.
>   So I sat still and touched nothing.

Who's to say, but perhaps in the next phase of Wright's career he must risk that touch, that change beyond knowing, must risk becoming one of his own constituency, "by their old ways forsaken / And startled on." And so—in the spirit of someone slipping a (now defunct) St. Christopher into the hand of a friend setting off on a journey—I'll close with Wright's own words:

> The problem with all of us as we get older is that we begin writing as though we were somebody. One should always write as if one were nobody. . . . We should always write out of our ignorance and desire and ambition, never out of some sense of false well-being, some tinge of success. There is no success in poetry, there is only the next inch, the next hand-hold out of the pit.[3]

Subject Matters

~~~~~

Inklings, Second Sights,
Chance Encounters

Given their many dissimilarities, accounts of how poems
come into being remain, at best, inconclusive, and what follows will
simply add to the assortment. That said, it has been my experience
that whatever opposite appearance it assumes, a poem's first journey
is outside in: it begins in time and history then labors to create a time
of its own, a time measured out in the shifting cadences of human
speech. Equally at odds with appearances, the "subject matter" of a
poem is, more often than not, uncalled for; like Hamlet's father, it
determines the time, place, and nature of its appearance. And even after the imagination has taken it in, has claimed it as an idée fixe, it
remains at liberty to determine when, and if, it submits itself to the
shaping method of "Words, words, words."

Since 1982, I've kept what I call a day-book. It's not a diary, not
quite a journal, not really a commonplace book either. It has served
instead as a gathering place for chance encounters of one sort or another, encounters which, however obliquely and in whatever incipi-
ent form, have suggested to me a kinship with poetry. I can't say
exactly what that kinship is; in fact, for many of these moments the
appeal resides in the degree to which—like those familiar objects
made suddenly strange in the space of a Cornell box—they resist
such explanations.

On the whole the entries tend less toward the aphoristic and declarative than toward the sidelong, overheard, and illusive. They in-

clude snippets of conversation, fleeting thoughts, fragments of mood and memory, perceptions and misperceptions, takes and double-takes, the *omnium gatherum* of everyday life. And while some have found their way into poems, others maintain the unassimilated shine of a shard of glass. What follows is a sampling, arranged in no particular order, selected to convey some feel for the wholly haphazard spirit in which they've presented themselves to me.

In the hospice gardens, midday in the bright sun, a woman of thirty or thirty-five, too weak, exhausted, or disinclined to walk the few yards back to her room raises her pale blue hospital gown and in one slow motion squats along the pathway to pee. And standing there beside her, her hopelessly embarrassed father, unable to look, unable not to look.

•

The flowering robe of a woman in Hilo (how many years ago?) who served me soup in a noodle shop where someone had bled on the floor.

•

A way of walking that leads people to mistake him for a child; and a child who, when I ask what he's writing, says, "I'm writing to improve my self of steam."

•

In India, I'm told, everyone prays to whomever they like, where, when, and how they like; and so, on occasion, it has happened that the milestones of the old French trading posts, because of their resemblance to the phallic emblems of Shiva, have been turned into altars by the passersby. Poetic imagination: an India of the mind.

•

In the middle of describing how it felt to discover his wife was having an affair, he glances hurriedly around the room, vainly in search of a comparison.

•

Writing about the past: the more I write, the more fictionalized the events become, until it seems I'm no longer seeking "the past" but trying to make the past more interesting. (So that I can better identify with it?)

◆

Language as a kind of clarity in which one sentence calmly engenders another, in which the meaning—fleeting, evanescent, perceptible only in the gentle modulations of the syllable-sounds—is something that surprises the writer as much as it does the reader.

◆

How often it seems some hidden nostalgia (the one for the little boy who lives down the lane?) expresses itself in the form of regret: "The man I might have been if I had not been the child I was." (Camus's *Notebooks*)

◆

I'm surprised to discover that, even in her early photographs, she wore that same expression—what her mother now calls her "thoughtful look"—the expression she assumes when faced with unwelcome scrutiny. An expression intended to erase all traces of who she is, and of how she feels at the moment.

◆

The self-reflective nature of law? In a Supreme Court ruling, Chief Justice Rehnquist describes a statute, which he considers prejudicial and outdated, as "a flower that blushes even in your absence."

◆

One by one throughout the day, each of the emptied garbage cans is lifted back up and carried inside (as only the truly forgiven can be).

◆

The groundskeeper in a churchyard cemetery stops his mower to explain: The headstones all face east so that, on the day of Judgment, the dead will rise up and fly directly into heaven. But a local, "unspoken" custom has it that wives whose husbands have been unfaithful will bury their men face down, so that, on the day of Judgment, they'll be flung directly into hell.

◆

For the last few days the overwhelming feeling (from the new medication?) that I've entered "a second phase" in my life. In the first it seemed I dreamed about life; in the second it seems life dreams about me.

♦

Sentences so stark and irreducible they seem almost complete as "works": "The olives had been painted from the asylum at St. Rémy in 1889." (A. S. Byatt, *Still-Life*)

♦

The strong impression that the "truth" about her is not to be found in the things she says, as if the things themselves, once they're spoken, assumed a life of their own. Hence, as in a childhood game of hide-and-seek—or, for that matter, as in a poem—whatever of her one hopes to find must be sought instead in the skulking shadow-life behind her words.

♦

Napoleon confessed that he'd rather have been the author of *Werther* than the emperor of Europe. The soft spot in the tyrant's heart (like Hitler's German shepherds), a warm place to curl up in the carnage.

♦

The endless bickering about "content" versus "experience" in a work of art. Can anyone listening to a recording of Mahalia Jackson's gospel songs talk about their content?

♦

From that day forward he consciously set out to be *different*. He decided to dress up every day, not to impress people, and not to fool them either—for telling the truth and telling a lie now shared a single purpose—but to bolster the odds against his failure. From that day forward his identity was largely rhetorical: *who he was* was simply a matter of *what he persuaded others of*. He became, as it were, a literary character.

♦

What would happen if, in place of the sufferings poets had experienced, they wrote about the sufferings they'd inflicted?

♦

An elderly woman on the flight from Heathrow. After our breakfast trays are removed, she rummages through the seat pocket in front of her, then turns to ask if perhaps I have "an extra body bag."

◆

A Belfast classroom in a predominantly Protestant secondary school, the blackboard deeply pocked from where, whenever the teacher turns his back, students hurl chunks of rock and scrap metal.

◆

Over tea the owner of the cottage in Greencastle (a member of the volunteer rescue team) describes how water in fishermen's waders will drag them down but keep them upright on the ocean bottom, "like a stand of oil-skinned kelp."

◆

Why complicate what is simple? The middle of the night, the prison lights across Lough Foyle, and Anna asleep on a folding cot, her radio headphones still turned on.

◆

I'm afraid I don't make a very good reader of literary biographies, for when I've finished one it's not the feel for the life I savor, but the odd and oftentimes meaningless detail: that the character of Heathcliff was based on the greatest love in Emily Bronte's life, her dog; that Proust's younger brother wrote a book called *The Surgery of the Female Genitalia* and was so celebrated for his prostatectomies that in the trade they were known as "*proust*atectomies"; that while at Vassar Elizabeth Bishop kept beside her bed a large jar of Roquefort, which she ate from before sleep in order to give herself better dreams; that with only the slightest pause in between, as "a singer takes a second breath," Gide was capable of achieving orgasm seven or eight times in succession . . . etc., etc.

◆

While admiring the polish and virtuosity of an older poet, I suddenly yearn for the harshness and indiscretion of a younger one.

◆

No matter how good the movie or lecture or concert may be, I find I can't take my eyes off anyone around me who starts falling asleep—

as though, in that battle between sleep and consciousness, the great drama of human existence were played out bravely before me.

◆

Did he misspeak, or did I mishear? "The multiple skulls of our handyman, Hans."

◆

Thinking back to his early reviews, the writer in Fitzgerald's "Afternoon of an Author" reflects how, "at the beginning fifteen years ago when they said he had 'fatal facility' . . . he labored like a slave over every sentence so as not to be like that."

◆

That rush of well-being when the headache passes, as if I'm suddenly filled with new thoughts.

◆

Sense and sensibility: "I learned very quickly to distinguish between the reality of thought and the reality of effects. But without this confusion is one a poet?" (Valéry, "A Poet's Notebook")

◆

"But it's not like that at all," she says. "With the baby there's a sense of being body-to-body, of being eaten *at* rather than eaten *of.*" She's explaining this with no trace of malice, in that peaceful hour before the lamp's turned off. "There's this sense of the baby drawing something from me without consuming me at the same time. With the baby, I never have that feeling I'm being dispossessed of some part of myself."

◆

An old man in a track suit hunches as he jogs at a pace a little slower than one might walk, his forehead shining in the sun.

◆

One of the more fascinating (and annoying) things about reading Stevens: the feeling that one is being trained to read. That, like Crispin, one is serving a "grotesque apprenticeship to chance event."

◆

A boy in his second grade class who refuses to speak, a boy he describes as completely "outsane."

◆

This evening, because I didn't answer the phone, L. burst into tears and ran out into the yard. When I went out to talk to her, she was sitting on the front steps smoking, and I suddenly remembered Flaubert's description of Rosanette in *Sentimental Education:* "She displayed a certain melancholy every night before going to bed. It was like finding cypress trees outside the door of a tavern."

◆

After-work traffic: the pilgrim trail of car-lights pours in slow procession down the valley floor.

◆

An emotion I can't seem to find any more, like a small misplaced object.

◆

A person who, if you mention a book that he dislikes and you admire, feels stupid. And a person who, under the same circumstances, does everything he can to make you feel stupid.

◆

She leaves before the second act of the Children's Theater Workshop, having felt as physically painful their "morbid attempts" to impress the adults in the audience.

◆

Emotions which lend themselves easily to poems: love, regret, self-adoration, wonder, languor, nostalgia. Emotions which prove resistant: docility, wholesomeness, optimism, self-control, diffidence, civility, incuriousness.

◆

While staying in Atlanta, I drive my mother to the V.A. Hospital to visit her brother. When we arrive on the Alzheimer's ward, we find him sitting in the activities room. He has a piece of food hanging from his chin and, as my mother bends to kiss him, it transfers from his chin to hers.

◆

One of the men on the ward carries a teddy bear, which he pets and cuddles and whispers to. Another talks to the ceiling in quick, explosive fragments. Yet another sits before a large, hand-printed sign with blank spaces where information is inserted. The sign says: "Today is *Friday.*" And below that: "Today is the *19th* of *August.*" But in fact "today" is Saturday, the 20th of August. The man in front of the sign keeps shouting, "Friday! Is today Friday? Is today the 19th of August?"

⬥

Frost's claim that every poem is a triumph of the human spirit over the materialism by which we're being overrun. Is it still possible to believe such things? A more credible triumph: Proust's habit of tipping as much as two hundred per cent of the restaurant bill.

⬥

Once they started seeing each other they were no longer the people I'd known before. His gestures became brusquer, smaller, more abstract, like the gestures of a marionette, while hers grew halting and self-conscious, wholly out of synch with his. It was as if the director of their relationship had made a bad choice in casting them.

⬥

During a lull in business, the bartender comes over to tell me about a sign in the embalming room of a funeral parlor where he used to work: "Please put babies on top shelf."

⬥

—"What makes you act the way you do?"
—"What do you mean by *that?*"
—"You know what I mean. The way you act, the way you are."
—"The way I am? How am I?"
—"You see, you're doing it again."
—"Doing what?"
—"Pretending you don't know what I'm talking about."
—"Oh, I know what you're talking about all right, I just don't know what you mean."
—"Really? Then why are you talking to me that way?"
—"It's you who's talking to *me* that way."

—"What way? What way am *I* talking to *you!*?"

◆

Suddenly in the last few weeks shifts in the weather are anathema to me, as if the rain, wind, snow, and cold, like the backdrops for a melodrama, conspired to intensify my feelings. But is this really so unlike—or unlike, perhaps, only by degree—how everyone is affected by the weather? Aren't people always taking it personally (especially poets)? "Deep sky is, of all visual impressions, the nearest akin to a feeling." (*Anima Poetae*)

◆

How compliantly, almost coweringly, people in the National Gallery respond to the commands of the guards—"step back," "don't touch," "no photographs," etc. No less so, I notice later, at the Holocaust Museum.

◆

It seems not only likely but unavoidable that a poem's reader has a different and more complicated relationship to the text than the poem's writer. What the reader sees includes the poet—those ever-shifting moods and emotions, quirks and dissemblings, flickering like candlelight behind the words—an advantage (over him- or herself) the poet never has.

◆

The funeral home's custom of donating flowers which adorn the caskets to a nearby nursing home—"to bring them a little cheer," the director explains. The very same flowers used to bury the dead are thereafter used to buoy up the spirits of the dying. But how terribly confused the flowers must be.

◆

For over an hour, while we sat and talked, their teenage daughter waited in the hallway for her friends to arrive. Then, at the sound of car tires on the gravel drive, she pulled her collar around her neck as if, inside, it had started to snow.

◆

Awakened from a deep sleep by the sound of my parents' love-making—which turns out to be the sound of L.'s asthmatic breathing beside me.

◆

All across town the parking-lot lights are just coming on. A ragged feel of snow in the air.

◆

At a party following his reading, the poet lets drop Schopenhauer's remark that life is like a child's shirt, "short and beshitted"—which, instead of the calculated effect (laughter? adulation? the knowing nod?), reduces everyone to silence. Perhaps there's more to be said for late-twentieth-century skepticism than we like to admit.

◆

Walking with L. beside the river: A gust of wind, and it's as if the world's been stirred to life by a phantom emotion we fear won't last, or won't last long, knowing our reluctance to assume such things.

◆

The moderator for a poetry reading at a widely publicized "avant-garde event" interrupts one reader to reproach the noisy crowd: "If you want to be offended, you'd better shut up!"

◆

Like a scene in Brueghel: late evening in the Arennes de Lutece, children frolicking in the sandpits and swings, mothers and nannies splayed out exhausted on the wooden benches, the plane trees glittered by a low-lying sun.

◆

The widespread, often willful reluctance to acknowledge how physical poetry can be—the raw, explicit carnality of it.

◆

Philip Larkin's famous remark about deprivation being to him what daffodils were to Wordsworth; and yet, one doesn't read Larkin for that deprivation alone (after all, deprivation is as common as the daffodil these days) but for the dream, the endless dream that flows from his work—like that "high-builded cloud" in "Cut Grass," "moving at summer's pace."

◆

At a restaurant, how slowly the life seems to drain from her face as, bite by bite, her lipstick smudges away.

◆

What a refreshing alternative: the familial, throat-slitting blood sport of Irish literary affairs.

◆

Not wanting to be worshipped as Gods but emulated as men, Buddha, Christ, Muhammad, and Socrates all refused to write anything down. But humanity stubbornly refuses to go any further in self-development.

◆

Yesterday, while driving home through an unseasonably cold October evening, I caught myself talking with my sister—more easily in my mind than I could to her face—when I suddenly remembered: *But she is dead.* And just saying those words brought a shock of unexpected tears. A shock I naively attributed to the *bitter* cold, the *cloudless* sky, the *deeply drifted* leaves.

◆

When I think about giving up writing, it's never for very noble reasons (whatever those might be) but from boredom, futility, hopelessness: "What Jules de Noailles said . . . is true: 'You will see one day that it is hard to speak about anything with anyone.'" (Jean Cocteau)

◆

The consoling, nearly unconscious feeling that day by day we grow further apart, that our apartness is a form of intimacy, and that the intimacy brings with it a heady intoxication I remember as the experience of "falling in love": that sense of the unknowability, the otherness, the absolute strangeness of another soul.

◆

X's style: A face that, as it ages, seems less a birthright than a curio.

◆

A childhood house I have written about, and that strange disjunction between the place itself and the place that I've described—as if somewhere along the line I'd written reality away.

◆

A dream in which a series of violent crashing sounds ends in a sudden silence, "like the silence of death." A moment later I awaken to that same silence, and for an hour or so I lie there, L. curled up beside me, as if together we waited, poised at the brink of oblivion, the dawn slowly breaking through the trees.

◆

In the middle of the essay—overwhelmed by the task before him?—Valéry suddenly interrupts himself to address his reader: "(I'm explaining myself as best I can.)"

◆

The more earnest and true they were with each other, the more they felt like they were living a kind of fairy tale—one with sinister overtones and an unhappy ending—and they longed for the days of secrecy and deception.

◆

—"I'm not going to harass you about it."
—"About what?"
—"About what you were talking about."
—"You're not going to harass me about it! What is there to harass me about?"
—"Nothing."
—"I thought you weren't going to harass me."
—"I'm not."
—"Aren't those tears I hear?"

◆

Poetry and the past? The Romantic view: poetry as invocation (*speak, memory*). The modern view: poetry as evocation (*speaking memory*). The postmodern view: poetry as recreation (*memory-speak*).

◆

July night, open window, no moon. And how I would like to exchange one thing (my life, perhaps) for the minute-driven nothingness that lies beyond the circle of the reading lamp.

◆

At the very moment the plane lifts off, a peace descends, the earth beneath those paling clouds slips beyond my reach. But when banking to land two hours later, that peace surrenders to a pang of fear, an odd, enervating, homesick fear. The thought of crashing? Or of returning to where my life left off?

◆

A poet who for years has been trying unsuccessfully to get his manuscript published. During that time his judgment of other poets has grown increasingly harsh and dismissive: "Yeats is the only poet I can read anymore." One morning he calls to say his manuscript has been accepted, and during the course of that conversation he recommends several new books of poetry, lavishing generous praise on each of them.

◆

One need only take a small step back, and the room in which the scholar delivering her paper, "a Lacanian reading of Henry James," becomes, in itself, a "Jamesian reading of Jacques Lacan."

◆

Moments when I can feel my memory falter, as if I'd called upon it to perform a function beyond its ordinary duties. And those moments just after, when I feel I'm trying to make amends by focussing my attention on whatever is presently before me: for example, the state of my faltering memory.

◆

And how like absence to surprise me this way: The tail-end of October, and children on bicycles trailing home through the curbside leaves.

◆

After the miscarriage, she appears to recover well, but then, increasingly, she can feel that loss passed back through her "like mud passed back by tunnelers in the dark."

＊

When, as a writer, one returns to childhood, one always returns in the role of the parent—dictatorial, revisionist, prescriptive, and prone to confuse the child with oneself.

＊

The moon tonight rising from the pines like a bus arriving at its terminus.

＊

The degree to which American culture continues to pander to the idea (or the fear) that Europeans "are far more interested in American barbarism [i.e., Buffalo Bill] than they are in American civilization." (Oscar Wilde)

＊

This morning at the hospice, while my grandmother rested, one of the nurses appeared in the doorway, tilted his head sideways and closed his eyes. I shook my head *no* to indicate that she wasn't dead, though I quickly realized he was only asking if she was sleeping. I've been here every day for two weeks and still confuse the signs of concern as signs of nosiness or insensitivity.

＊

On the moveable table beside her bed, a button which reads "Vanity Release."

＊

Unable any longer to speak or hear or even move her head, she opens her eyes and stares at me. And then, very slowly, at the corner of one eye, a tear begins to form, in sadness or pain I couldn't say. It seems to take forever, though no matter how long it fills it simply will not fall.

＊

The body: A bright room through which the shadow of a bird has just passed.

＊

Kafka's impression that in any communication which passes through space (letters, telephone, radio, etc.) some human element gets drunk along the way by a gathering community of ghosts. A nourishment on which their community thrives, for the ghostly distance between people grows ever larger in time.

In a Glass, Darkly

Reflections on Contemporary
American Poetry

During a year in which my wife and son and I were living in
Paris, I was required to spend a few weeks in bed recovering from an
illness. A little time in sickbed can sometimes be a pleasant thing, and
we were lucky enough to have a friend who showed up at our apartment every few days with an armload of new things to read. On one
particular morning that armload consisted of a small stack of poetry
journals from America, and I can still remember, as she set them
down on the bedside table, the momentary pall that passed over me:
A quick glance revealed there wasn't a novel in the bunch, and the
covers looked all too familiar and glum.

Or did they? While our first months away had felt blissfully removed from "the poetry world," those journals awakened a curiously
heartfelt nostalgia (a nostalgia I dared not confess at the time) for the
untiring, untidy, and mildly incestuous busyness of that world. What
I was pleased to recall is not only the scale of interest that exists in
American poetry today (well beyond its counterpart in France) but
also the lacerating fervor with which those interests are defended,
disregarded, anatomized, and abhorred. Any art, like any government,
is better off for the give-and-take of spirited debate, the free-for-all
of self-examination—and our poetry appears to have plenty of that.

Perhaps because those things were running through my head, I took
special notice of one particular set of complaints that kept cropping
up, with the nagging persistence of a guilty conscience, in the pages

I was reading. These were the same complaints, more or less, that I'd been hearing for years from poets and critics alike, and they all seemed to issue from the largely unexamined, but nonetheless shared, assumption that contemporary American poetry, its vital functions shot, is somehow unnaturally kept alive by the machinery of academic life-support: namely, the creative writing workshops.

But even if we were to concede the basis for this judgment (the recent spawn of creative writing programs?), we must still confront one obdurate fact: the prodigious, nearly incalculable diversity of contemporary American poetry confounds all attempts to lump it under any one label, or charge, or description. From the Black Aesthetics of Askia Muhammad Touré to the Steinian poetics of Charles Bernstein, from the *engagement* of Adrienne Rich to the *dégagement* of John Ashbery, from the canonical authority of the *Harper's Anthology of Twentieth-Century Native American Poetry* to the defensive neoclassicism of the New Formalists, from Miguel Algarín's *Voices from the Nuyorican Poets' Café* to the Cowboy traditions of Howard "Jack" Thorp and Bruce Kiskaddon, from the hip-hop rhythms of rap to the haphazard rhythms of the poetry slam . . . It may be more accurate to call it, not "contemporary American poetry" at all, but "contemporary American poetries."

Still, in the face of that abundance, the complaint persists, and curiously enough it appears to have intensified at a time when our poetry is undergoing the very kind of public revival which saves it from academic confinement. Not only has the mainstream begun (reluctantly or not) to open its doors to a widening range of marginalized poets, but the last two decades have seen a flurry of broad-based poetry activities: the establishment of a national poetry month; formal White House celebrations of poetry hosted by the President and First Lady; the appearance in Los Angeles of billboards filled with poems by contemporary poets; the inclusion of a poetry book as a "standard feature" with all new Volkswagens shipped in April; a cross-country book giveaway inspired by Joseph Brodsky's winning avowal that poetry should be as available as the Gideon Bible; the distribution by tollbooth operators in New Jersey of free copies of Whitman's "Leaves of Grass"; the proliferation of poetry awards, web sites, spoken-arts recordings, open-mike nights, and public radio and television specials . . . to name just a few.

So what lies behind our troubled conscience? Is it a peculiarly American neurosis, I wondered, to be hungry for general acceptance but not wanting to be caught receiving it? True as that may be, it doesn't account for the particulars of those recurring complaints, nor does it explain their persistence and uniformity. Perhaps because I was living in Paris, where the politics of culture assigns such problems to the critical theorists, I felt a surge of that peculiar brand of American pragmatism which says, If you want to get to the bottom of this, you'd better roll up your sleeves and dig.

The complaints, I notice, tend to cluster around four main points: (1) we have too many poets; (2) we have no great poets; (3) there is a sameness to all our poems; and (4) our poems aren't sufficiently engaged in issues of immediate political or social concern. As everyone knows, those assertions are so commonplace it hardly seems necessary to attach them to any one person. But for the sake of specificity, I'll refer when necessary to two recent essays, essays I've chosen because they're both intelligent and persuasive, because together they raise all the issues I've listed, and because one is written by a poet, the other by a social and literary critic (and so, one assumes, these are matters of general concern): respectively, Donald Hall's "Poetry and Ambition" and Terrence Des Pres's "Self / Landscape / Grid." Another reason I've selected these two is because they're both reprinted in *The Pushcart Prize, IX: Best of the Small Presses,* so they've been rightly acknowledged for the integrity of their ideas, even though *Pushcart* is, as its subtitle suggests, a manifestation of the phenomenon they criticize.

(1) There are too many poets.
What does it mean to say there are too many poets? It's a strange assertion, to be sure, though it's something one hears a lot and, I was

pleased to discover, not only in this decade. Yeats was addressing similar concerns before the Rhymers' Club at the turn of the century; Coleridge was sensitive to a growing and gloomy kind of competitiveness; and given the number of poets in America today, one suspects that Plato would've felt the Republic was coming under siege. But to say there are "too many" suggests some crisis the numbers don't fully explain. It suggests some erosive, softening effect the numbers are having on our poetry overall.

It seems an obvious if often overlooked point that the value of poetry in any age will be gauged by the best poets of that period and not by the rest. To say there are too many poets, then, would seem meaningless unless those numbers had somehow conspired to enact a version of Emperor Gratian's law: the bad drive out the good. And the proof of *that*, I suppose, could only be established by demonstrating a dearth of "greatness" in our day. We'll come back to the issue of greatness in section two, but for the moment let's ask: Okay, so what's the problem with having all these people writing poems, all these people who may never be Sappho or Dante or Shakespeare— or, for that matter, the next winner of the local poetry prize?

For centuries in China it was common practice for lovers to exchange poems instead of letters. In seventeenth-century England most educated people could turn out a fairly competent sonnet to celebrate some occasion or another. And just to take a more personal example, when my grandmother died we discovered among her letters a thin volume of twelve poems, one for each month of the first year of her marriage, which she'd written and had privately printed as an anniversary gift for my grandfather. Parts of the poems were surprisingly good (I recall one passage in particular, about "the sunlight washing soap smell" of his hair), other parts were predictable, sentimental, eager to please, certainly none of them approached (except perhaps in my grandfather's mind) that quality we refer to as "greatness." That said, it's difficult to see the harm in all this less-than-great poetry. As Philip Larkin once famously remarked, "Supposing no one played tennis because they wouldn't make Wimbledon." Whatever the literary value of my grandmother's poems, they still seemed to be written, to my mind anyway, for the best of reasons: because it gave her and at least one other person pleasure to do so.

I wonder, too, if the relationship between poetry and the "amateur poets" (if that's what we must call them) isn't enhanced by the practice of composition. I can recall at the age of nineteen or twenty the strangely exalted feeling I had as I was working my way through my first "serious" sonnet. The feeling that, through the enduring mysteries of that age-old form, I was somehow drawing closer in understanding to the sonnets of Helen Hunt Jackson, Robert Frost, Claude McKay, and (that subversively loyal sonneteer) e. e. cummings, the models I'd chosen to emulate. It finally didn't matter, or didn't matter too much, that my own poem plodded woodenly along in lines studiously remote from any language I'd ever spoken. It didn't matter because I'd learned a little more about the extraordinary subtlety and complexity of the form, and hence about the extraordinary accomplishment of Jackson's "Poppies on the Wheat," Frost's "Never Again Would Birds' Song Be the Same," McKay's "Harlem Dancer," and cummings's "[you shall above all things be glad and young]," each a personal favorite at the time. I was learning something more about how those poems were made, and I was learning as well about the imagination and intuition and technical skill (not to mention the plain good luck) that must all come together for a sonnet to succeed. From having tried it myself, I better understood what cummings meant: "I'd rather learn from one bird how to sing / than teach ten thousand stars how not to dance."

But doesn't that, or some variation of that happen any time anyone seriously undertakes to compose a poem, however modest the undertaking? What I'm getting at is this: The apparent abundance of poets may not have led to an abundance of great poets (the terms "abundance" and "great" don't seem to go together in any period), but if nothing else it has given rise to a richer understanding of, and a more refined sensitivity to, poetic language and its effects. At least larger than would exist otherwise.

All that may sound as if I've conceded the fact that we're living in a time when great poems have ceased being written. But before we take up that issue, I'd like to sound the precautionary note that Palgrave issued in his 1897 preface to *The Golden Treasury: Second Series:* "Nothing, it need scarcely be said, is harder than to form an estimate even remotely accurate of our own contemporary artists."

(2) There are no great poets.

This complaint has many variants, though the two most popular appear to be that today's poets lack ambition and that our poems lack both the depth and scale which poetry once possessed. In support of this, people are fond of quoting things like Keats's "I shall be among the English poets after my death" or (this is Hall's choice) "I would sooner fail than not be among the greatest." These remarks are intended to say, See, how many poets say *that* these days? But surely those sorts of remarks in the mouth of anyone other than Keats run the risk of sounding pretty silly. (Consider Eliot's habit of clearing his throat with phrases like "Virgil and I . . . ") And one suspects that our deference to Keats has as much to do with the heartbreaking circumstances of his life and death as it does with any exemplary ambition. For it's also true that, in one of his periodic swings of mood, Keats decided he would only write for money: "The very corn which is so beautiful, as if it had only took to ripening yesterday, is for the market."

More often than not ambition is tied to some (no doubt fleeting) feeling of self-certainty, and as poets soon discover, self-certainty is a card the muses are quick to trump. John Berryman once glumly observed that no poet will ever know the real value of his or her work. And I'd be surprised to find that any poet who has spent a lifetime writing hasn't thought, at one time or another, both "I shall be among the greats" and "nothing I've written is worth a damn." The one tends to keep the other in check.

But why aren't there any great poets? both Hall and Des Pres have asked. In Hall's mind, "It seems to me that contemporary American poetry is afflicted by modesty of ambition—a modesty, alas, genuine." He then acknowledges that "the great majority of poems, in any era, will always be bad or mediocre"; and he follows that with: "We fail in part because we lack serious ambition." The implication, then, is that, not only are the "great majority" of our poems unambitious, but so are those which in other times would have distinguished themselves from the majority.

As with the first complaint, I wonder about the basis for such conclusions. For example, does it take into account the contemporaneous publication of Adrienne Rich's *Your Native Land, Your Life*, about which the poet herself declared the Whitmanesque goal "to speak from, and of, and to my country. To speak a different claim from those staked by the patriots of the sword"? Or Robert Pinsky's *An Explanation of America*, a book whose ambition is asserted in the bravado of its title? Or James Merrill's epic trilogy-in-verse, *The Changing Light at Sandover*, a book which, at 560 pages in length, is comparable in scale to any poetry of any time? There are any number of books which, for a variety of reasons, might be added to this list, but keeping Palgrave's caution in mind, I don't intend to make a case for the "greatness" of any single work, or even for my personal preferences. Instead, in the hopes of providing at least some particulars for a counter-claim to Hall's assertion—that our poetry is afflicted by "a modesty of ambition"—I would like to focus on *The Changing Light at Sandover*. Whatever one might feel about the ultimate value of Merrill's book, its ambition is easy enough to gauge.

The matter of its length aside, the ideas in the trilogy range from extended speculations on the apocalyptic march of Western civilization to packed dramatizations of the most abstruse mystical and scientific theories; its materials include Ouija-encoded telegrams laid alongside a carefully orchestrated dialogue of voices which run the gamut of intellectual and literary history; and through a spiraling ladder of formal structures (which summon the pattern of a DNA molecule, the central trope throughout) the level of its language shifts from the demotic to the grand, from the sociable to the oracular, from the whispered to the proclaimed. Furthermore, the entire set of comedies Merrill calls divine is refigured in a system of cosmic scale overseen by a God (the God Biology) who's as credible in our century as Dante's and Milton's was in theirs.

Given all that, one might reasonably wonder why Merrill isn't mentioned, favorably or not, in Hall's essay. Instead, he spends an awful lot of time decrying what he (perhaps too easily) calls the "McPoem," the poem "the workshop schools us to produce." As we all know, the "workshop" makes a large and popular target, to the point where the term has come to denote a single method of teaching, no matter the place, the teacher, or the student. It's as though the term "drama class" were used to refer to a single play being acted out the same way everywhere. Even so, the "workshop poem" (whatever that is) could hardly be considered indicative of, or representative of, the best being written today, any more than the rash of so-called Imagist poems were of the best being written in the 1920s. I return to Hall's earlier remark: "*Of course* the great majority of poems, in any era, will always be bad or mediocre."

That said, I like to think there's another side to this issue. I like to think that a case could be made for poets giving up ambition altogether, or at least the kind that's inclined to announce (Hall's words again): "The grander goal is to be as good as Dante." While it's hard to argue against Dante being a grander goal—the massive potential for writer's block aside—perhaps we could entertain an alternative approach, the approach one finds exemplified in the peculiar genius of Elizabeth Bishop. If any one person were going to serve as a model for younger poets, I think she'd make a pretty good choice, and I can't imagine her saying anything even remotely like, "I should sooner fail than not be among the greatest."

In a writing life that spanned more than fifty years, Bishop published just over ninety poems. There are no epics, no poems of elaborate or showy technical experiment, there's nothing that requires an academic guide, nothing to make a reader feel inferior to the text. In fact, her poems seem completely free of that desire to be as great as someone else or to make their mark on the world of literature. And yet, of course, the mark they've left is both large and indelible.

So what are we to make of her ambition? And how is ambition to be gauged? By quantity? Scale? Innovation? The necessity of interpretive assistance? Those features characteristic of what Ned Rorem has called, referring to Wagner, "the masterpiece syndrome"? Recent feminist criticism has had edifying things to say about the different ways "ambition" is manifest in male and female writers, and the aforementioned attributes settle too easily on the masculine side. By contrast, Bishop's coolly clairvoyant poems seem removed altogether from the blood-sport of literary ambition. And if one must settle on the term "ambition" as a substitute for literary excellence, then one must (in her case anyway) locate it somewhere else: in the overriding impression that she writes, not from the drive for literary conquest, but from the urgent and wholly private thrill of artistic necessity.

One further point worth considering. If a poet is possessed of a particular kind of genius, that genius will no doubt manifest itself, to some degree, in poems of any scale. But it's also possible that the sensibility of that particular person may be better suited to a smaller scale. This was the case, I think, with Bishop in poetry, just as it was with Chekhov in fiction, Chopin in music, Vermeer in painting, and Cornell in his assemblages. Conversely, if a poet is without genius, that too will show itself in poems of any scale, and it's not going to matter that he or she sets out with all the ambition in the world to write another *Iliad* or *Paradise Lost.*

(3) *There is a sameness to all the poems today.*
This complaint seems to derive from a confusion of numbers, and because of that it's the least interesting of the four. There are, I think, two equations responsible. First, if you have ten poets—one great, two good, and seven mediocre (that's no doubt high on the side of the good and great)—the seven mediocre poets are going to resemble each other by an absence of those distinguishing qualities which the other three possess. In the same way, I imagine my grand-

mother's poems resembled those poems exchanged by lovers in China, and many of the poems on a common theme in seventeenth-century England. But here again, the measure of any generation is made by its best poets, not the rest.

The second equation is equally straightforward. Given the same breakdown of ten poets, it seems likely, even healthy, that somewhere along the line the seven mediocre poets are going to notice what the other three are doing, and perhaps they'll attempt to do it themselves. This may lead to a particular period (and we all know of such periods) when as many as eight or nine of the ten appear to be writing the same poem; but even on casual reading I'd think one could distinguish the imitators from the originals. And isn't it possible that, when those three poets become aware of their imitators, they'll be far less tempted by self-imitation?

To put it more bluntly, if there were only ten poets in America, the proportions wouldn't bother anyone. But because there are thousands, it must seem that there's more mediocrity than ever. My guess is that there's no more now than there ever was.

(4) Our poems aren't sufficiently engaged in matters of immediate political or social concern.
The question of the political role the poet plays has woven a loose thread through the history of literature, and one need only tug it once to quickly divide the tapestry. Clearly the old answers from both sides couldn't adequately account for the extraordinary predicament we've found ourselves facing in this century. A predicament so dire that a remark like Auden's "poetry makes nothing happen" (however misrepresented it is) evokes an almost reflexive response: "Well, it better start to, and fast."

The question then becomes: What, if anything, can poetry *make happen?* Perhaps we can begin to formulate an answer by posing some questions to the question itself. First, is poetry's nature (that is, what it *is* intrinsically) somehow different, or separable from, its function (what it *does* extrinsically)? If so, then what in its nature is, or should be, responsible to that function? And, by extension, would poetry divorced from function become, by definition, superficial and inessential to our lives? Conversely, if poetry's nature and function are one and the same thing, then wouldn't Auden's line be better understood, and more generally acceptable, if it read "Poetry makes nothing but poetry happen"? However one feels about these issues, they invariably give rise to that age-old division between the aesthetic and social responsibilities of art—and they inevitably end with each side arguing from the outpost of a wholly defensible position. But by such divisions we often overlook the common ground that both sides share.

Clearly, if we were to judge from modern history, poetry *by its mere existence* appears to embody a powerful political purpose, a purpose that, however unacknowledged in these discussions, has been obvious enough to the forces of power all over the globe. Time and again our century has shown that the tyrant, the dictator, the totalitarian government is deeply threatened by poetry. The record overflows with examples: Osip Mandelstam in Russia, Nazim Hikmet in Turkey, Wisława Szymborska in Poland, Jack Mapanje in Malawi, Bei Dao in China. . . .

But what in poets, one must ask, awakens in tyrants such murderous fears? Perhaps the very fact that poetry represents a deeply compelling alternative world to the one the tyrant controls. And lyric poetry in particular provides an alternative time as well, a time outside of history, outside the story upon which the tyrant has established his base of power. For one of the virtues poetry maintains is a belief in the possibility that human life, the life we lead from day to day, may be something more than a chore—or a terror. It imagines our experience in a state of heightened aliveness, in a state where things might suddenly happen to change us into a fuller and more exuberant version of ourselves. This is a secret poets seem to share with children, gamblers, drunks, and saints, and as long as the experience of an alternative world is kept alive, then we're able to measure the experience of our daily lives against an assortment of alternative experiences. It appears that poetry, great poetry anyway, exists somewhere beyond the orthodoxies of social and political life—and in so doing it stakes a very powerful claim against the leveling forces of totalitarianism.

With that in mind, we can address the particulars of Des Pres's complaint. I may be wrong about this, but my impression is that, however divided people may be about the political and aesthetic priorities of art, most would agree that it's dangerous to assume there's a single stipulated set of concerns which poetry—by nature or by conscience—is obliged to address. Because of that, it's unsettling to read things like, "I've just gone through the recent issue of *American Poetry Review*, which offers forty-eight poems . . . but only two touch upon our nuclear fate, which leaves forty-six in worlds elsewhere." This remark from Des Pres's article comes in support of his opinion that the poetry of our age—through indifference, irresponsibility, or willful ignorance—is insufficiently "informed by nuclear awareness." He prefaces his remarks by saying how much he loves poetry, and how he turns to it for "strength to endure." I don't question Mr. Des Pres's sincerity—the author of a remarkable book, *The Survivor: An Anatomy of Life in the Death Camps*, Des Pres has spent his life engaged with the darkest spiritual and political issues of our time— though I do question the process by which he arrives at this opinion, a process that leads him to imagine some scale of thematic proportion which one poem in twenty-four can't satisfy.

The dangers of such a conception of the arts are, unfortunately, quite real in this century. China and the Soviet Union, for example, have left a frightening record of what happens to the arts when they're monitored by, and enlisted to serve, the state. The results have proven anathema to the arts (not to mention civil liberties), whose "steady work," as John Hollander has observed, "is to save art from the false versions of itself that human institutions are continually spawning." All other questions aside, poets writing in a free state— free both politically and psychologically—tend to write those poems some inner compulsion urges them to write, not always those they'd like to write, not always those they attempt to write, and perhaps not often enough those they ought to write. But like it or not, that's the way that poems get written: out of the leverage which poems necessarily maintain over the conscious intentions of the poet. The poem, it turns out, has a mind of its own, and when poets start writing what they're told to write, or what they think they're supposed to write, the results inevitably belie that purpose, and we're left to ponder what Shakespeare called an "art tongue-tied by authority": the poem has exchanged experience for persuasion, instinct for purpose, intuition for intention.

And do we really want poetry to be "responsible," in the sense this argument intends? Responsible to what, one asks, and to whom? The polis? Culture? Society? Convention? Morality? Art? And who is going to decide? And once that argument is institutionalized, once art is held to the standard of "responsibility," hasn't history shown (Jesse Helms is a useful example here) that the "standard" becomes a tool for maintaining both the status quo and the ruling orthodoxies of the day? And at just such moments, isn't *irresponsibility* the very thing which poetry is called to provide? The very same kind of irresponsibility that Robert Mapplethorpe brought to photography? An irresponsibility to those very ideas which society employs to define itself and its citizens? Where would gay and lesbian writing be, for example, had it not been irresponsible to prevailing social norms? As Edmund White has observed, "Art and passion live, thrive and die regardless of public utility and convenience; art and passion are the two supremely irresponsible modes of experience."

And perhaps the idea that one can legislate, or coerce, or even imitate social conscience has a built-in sentimentality, a sentimentality well illustrated in an article by John Ashbery on the painter Fairfield Porter. Porter was attending a meeting of the Artists' Club on Eighth Street in New York, and the subject under discussion that evening was whether or not it was vain for artists to sign their paintings. The argument apparently went back and forth, each side vehemently defending its position, when someone finally called on Porter. "If you are vain," he responded, "it is vain to sign your paintings and vain not to sign them. If you are not vain, it is not vain to sign them and not vain not to sign them." The koan-like wisdom of Porter's response goes overlooked in much of the "political criticism" so popular these days. But the plain and unfortunate fact remains that if one is insensitive or cruel or bigoted or vain, one's actions will inevitably manifest those traits whatever opposite appearance they assume. And if every poet in America suddenly started writing poems on the subject of the nuclear threat, I suspect the predicament Des Pres describes would no more be altered than the souls of those painters had they suddenly stopped signing their paintings.

But does that mean that poetry is somehow excused from social obligation? Des Pres claims we've reached a crisis, "the spectacle of spirit cowed and retreating." He writes: "What's called for, in fact, is the kind of poetry we once named great," and he cites Wordsworth and Whitman as examples. Like others who make this claim, instead of addressing those poems written on the scale of Wordsworth or Whitman, he chooses to leaf through "a recent issue of *American Poetry Review*," and after that "I went on to *Poetry* . . . and after that I rummaged randomly through the library's stock of recent journals and magazines." (It's more than curious—it's a little alarming—that Des Pres never refers to a single book, and instead makes random rummaging the basis for his conclusion.) Here again we should keep in mind Hall's observation: "The great majority of poems, in any era, will always be bad or mediocre." And by that same right, the great majority of poets in any era will no doubt reflect the same moral attitudes, and the same degree of social responsibility, that one finds in the population at large. Where one must look, then—and especially if one is looking to poetry for "strength to endure"—is not to the great majority, but to that minority of the great. And to find them, one had better start reading less randomly, and one had better start reading some books.

Which brings us back to the matter of "greatness." It seems everyone harbors a slightly different version of what that is. For Des Pres it's those poems which "confront their times" and "face and contain their own negation." Specifically what he "hopes to see" is "poetry that probes the impact of nuclear threat, poetry informed by nuclear knowing, poems that issue from the vantage of a self that accepts its larger landscape, a poetic diction testing itself against the magnitude of our present plight, or finally just poems which survive their own awareness of the ways nuclear holocaust threatens not only mankind but the life of poetry itself" (*sic*).

Given the particularity of those concerns, I find myself again surprised by the fact that, like Hall, Des Pres never mentions *The Changing Light at Sandover*, a poem which addresses, not only the issue of the nuclear threat, but also the overarching question of energy, nuclear and otherwise. And not only energy's potential for destruction, but also our relationship to that energy, the ways in which we are energy (electrical in the human sphere, atomic in the divine), the ways in which energy serves as an integral part of our religious and cultural and literary myths, our biologies, our evolving physio-psychological systems. Accordingly, in the shorthand of a Ouija board, we learn that God Biology, who rules the universe, takes his power from the forge of nuclear energy: "THE FIRE THE FUEL OF THE PANTHEON OF THE GODS / OF THE VARIOUS GALAXIES GOD B GUARDS THIS POWER / JEALOUSLY IT IS HIS BRIGHT RED APPLE." In Promethean terms, we are stealing God's fire, and we are duly warned: "THIS TOO MUST CEASE / . . . THE ATOM MUST / BE RETURND TO THE LAB & THE USES OF PARADISE." [1]

Far from simply writing a poem "informed by nuclear knowing," Merrill has attempted to examine—among a host of other things, including a second great threat to our planet, overpopulation—the intimate and complex nature of the thing we've come to dread. Still, in his entire article Des Pres refers to Merrill only once, and then only as someone who, "like Yeats," "held some very odd convictions." Fair enough. But surely we can allow for the possibility that, in the arts, "odd convictions" may be nothing more than a descriptive phrase for the manner by which the accumulated wisdom of human history is filtered through the imagination: "PURE REASON / NOT IN THE VOL-

TAIREAN SENSE BASED ON KNOWLEDGE MERELY / BUT REASON RUN THRU
THE FIRES OF MAN'S CLONED SOUL."[2]

As Palgrave recognized, it's foolish to pretend we can gauge which, if any, of our contemporaries the future will consider great. But I'd like to suggest that an only slightly less frightening situation than not having a great poet when you need one is not recognizing (or even reading) a great poet when you have one. And just as we need great poets, we also need, as Whitman pointed out, great readers and great critics, those willing to confront those very same issues which Des Pres himself has outlined.

But setting the issue of "greatness" aside, I'd like to return to those thousands of poets (good, bad, and mediocre, amateur and professional alike) we have in America today. And I'd like to return by way of an anecdote from that period I spent in Paris. On Christmas Eve of that year, my wife and son and I were sitting around our two-room flat drinking hot chocolate, exchanging gifts, and trying unsuccessfully to tape a worn out pair of socks to the sill above the radiator. After they'd gone off to bed, I decided to catch the Métro over to Notre-Dame to watch the midnight Mass. For someone brought up in a decidedly casual, "freethinking" family, I'd visited an unusual number of churches, cathedrals, temples, and mosques, but on only a handful of occasions (and those, as I recall, against my will) had I attended actual services. Still, midnight Mass on Christmas Eve in one of the great cathedrals in the world had its own dramatic appeal.

It was just after eleven when I arrived, but already the enormous inner chamber was crowded with people, and hundreds more were streaming in through the vaulted doors. The votive candle stands at either side of the entryway were so over-filled that people had started melting candles onto the concrete railings of the side walls. The dozens of chandeliers that lined the aisles overflowed with lights as well, and all those lights and all those candles were muted and dimmed by incense issuing, in huge blue cumulus clouds, from two basins at the front of the altar.

By the time the Mass began, the air was growing uncomfortably thick, and those of us standing on the perimeter were packed in so tight that it was becoming difficult to move. On one side of me were a young north African man and woman with their infant child; on the other side, a Brazilian teenage girl with a bright knit cap she'd pulled down shyly over her ears; in front, a middle-aged Austrian couple; and behind, a short, plump, elderly woman (a Parisian grandmother, I later found out) who couldn't have seen beyond my shoulders. Like a group of strangers the fates had cast onto a rough sea in a shaky boat, our survival instincts took over. We each took turns holding the baby above our heads so that she or he (I never was quite sure) could get plenty of air. Still, more and more people poured into the cathedral, and tighter and tighter we were pressed together.

I'm not comfortable in crowds, and being packed in that way was beginning to make me (and the Parisian grandmother as well, I noticed) feel a little claustrophobic. But at just that point when the first bright, panicky flutters began to spread their wings, the cathedral organ droned out into the incensed air the opening chords of a familiar carol. And then, very gradually, in a swell that began at the front of the cathedral and moved in a wave toward the back, everyone began to sing: "*Gloria in excelsis Deo . . .*" For reasons that remain mysterious to me, it was only a matter of moments before my panic gave way to the singing, before the Parisian grandmother tapped me on the shoulder and smiled. For there we were, pressed side to side, back to front and front to back, so tightly packed that the sensation was not of singing alone, but of singing through everyone around you, and of everyone singing through you.

I suppose one could say the singing had, to borrow Des Pres's term, helped me to endure. And it's interesting to note that the words were in Latin, and even though I'd guess that few of us there understood their meanings, it was clear that it didn't really matter. It didn't really matter so much *what* we were singing—was it actually better we didn't know?—as the simple fact that we *were* singing. That through the heady combination of song and the human voice we were lifted momentarily beyond the confines of our individual selves (or fears, as the case may be).

It pleases me to think that something similar happens in poetry. As James Merrill has suggested, poetry remains one of three new faiths—music and science being the other two—still possible in our age. And it pleases me to think that in America today we have all of these thousands of people singing, and that, even if none of us is "as good as Dante," perhaps collectively we express some as-yet-unquenched spirit, some potential that's still important enough to slow our march toward self-destruction. Perhaps it's possible that the way poetry can "make something happen" is quite different from the way we've come to expect. And perhaps insufficient notice has been taken of this simple but unassailable truth: that however awkward and maladept, however grand and uplifting, it isn't just a matter of what we sing, or how well we sing, it's the quite remarkable fact that, in a century like ours, we've somehow managed to save from extinction that deep-down, fundamental desire to sing.

Notes

A Toy Balloon, the Man-Moth's Tear, and a Sack of Ripe Tomatoes

    1.   Salinger, *Seymour—An Introduction*, 128–29.

    2.   Salinger, *Seymour—An Introduction*, 119–20.

On the Memory of Stone

    1. Jeffers, foreword to *The Selected Poetry.*

    2. It needs to be said that, however fascinating Jeffers's collection of stones may be, one can't help question the impulse, perhaps even the ethics behind certain acquisitions: a rectangular stone "roughly carved with a cross . . . found lying in a little lane near Clondahorky church-yard, near Dunfanaghy, County Donegal, Ireland"; a Babylonian tile (circa 2100 B.C.) inscribed with a prayer to Ishtar; the carved stone head of an aspara from the temple of Prah-Khan in Cambodia; a fragment of ceramic from the Temple of Heaven in Peking; a cement plaque into which Jeffers set "bits from practically all of the ancient and mysterious round towers of Ireland." No explanation is offered in the monograph.

    3. It may be worth recalling that the ancient Greek word for "stone" comes from *Hermes*, god of doorways and portals, and that from this root we get our word "hermetic."

    4. Jeffers, *Selected Poetry*, 563, 605.

A Story of Poetry and Poets

    1. Sewell, *The Orphic Voice*, 41, 47.

    2. Barthes, *A Lover's Discourse*, 14.

    3. Barthes, *A Lover's Discourse*, 14.

    4. Ovid, *Metamorphoses*, 235.

    5. Ovid, *Metamorphoses*, 235.

6. Blanchot, "The Gaze of Orpheus," 99.

7. Blanchot, "The Gaze of Orpheus," 100.

8. Blanchot, "The Gaze of Orpheus," 100.

9. Ovid, *Metamorphoses*, 235.

10. Barthes, *A Lover's Discourse*, 29–30.

11. Calasso, *Marriage of Cadmus and Harmony*, 81.

12. Calasso, *Marriage of Cadmus and Harmony*, 80–81.

13. Ovid, *Metamorphoses*, 236.

14. Ovid, *Metamorphoses*, 236.

15. Cixous, *Three Steps on the Ladder of Writing*, 7.

16. Ovid, *Metamorphoses*, 236.

17. Ovid, *Metamorphoses*, 239.

18. Ovid, *Metamorphoses*, 261.

Writing the Poet, Unwriting the Poem

1. Eliot, *Complete Poems and Plays*, 139.

Shelley in Ruins

1. Wilde, *The Artist as Critic*, 366–67.

Eating the Angel, Conceiving the Sun

1. Heidegger, *What Is Called Thinking?*

2. Heidegger, *What Is Called Thinking?* 9, 17.

3. Heidegger, *What Is Called Thinking?* 6.

4. Rilke, *Letters of Rainer Maria Rilke*, 375–76.

5. Rilke, *Letters of Rainer Maria Rilke*, 87.

6. Heidegger, *What Is Called Thinking?* 8–9.

7. Heidegger, *What Is Called Thinking?* 6.

8. Heidegger, "The Thinker as Poet," 6.

9. Bishop, letter to Robert Lowell, 20 May 1955, Houghton Library, Harvard University.

10. Butts, *Conversations with Richard Wilbur*, 53–54.

11. Heidegger, *What is Called Thinking?* 11.

12. Rilke, *Letters*, 317.

13. Cixous, *Three Steps*, 7, 20.

14. Hendry, *Sacred Threshold*, 12.

15. Valéry, *The Art of Poetry*, 81.

"Into the Unknown to Find the New"

1. The Poets' House, where this essay was first delivered as a lecture, was an international school for poets in Northern Ireland (now resettled in the Republic); located on the coast of the Irish Sea, it looked east to Scotland and south to the Isle of Man.

2. Heidegger, "What are Poets For?" 91.

3. Kafka, "The Hunter Gracchus," 133, 135.

4. All quotations from Baudelaire are from Richard Howard's translation of *Les Fleurs du Mal*.

5. Valéry, *Art of Poetry*, 72.

6. Sartre, *Baudelaire*, 17.

7. Heidegger, *Poetry, Language, Thought*, 94.

8. Bachelard, *The Poetics of Space*, 5–6.

9. Sartre, *Baudelaire*, 166–67.

À la Recherche de la Poésie Perdue

1. Wordsworth, *Selected Poems and Prefaces*, 454.

2. Tomlinson, "The Presence of Translation," 258.

3. Quoted in Biguenet and Schulte, *The Craft of Translation*, ix.

4. Wordsworth, *The Prelude*, book IV, lines 290–91.

5. Wordsworth, *Selected Poems and Prefaces*, 456.

6. Warren, *The Art of Translation*, 3.

7. Wheatley, *Poems of Phillis Wheatley*, 6.

8. Johnson, "Taking Fidelity Philosophically," 142–43.

9. Burnshaw, *The Poem Itself*, xi–xiii.

10. Benjamin, "The Task of the Translator," 259.

11. Benjamin, "The Task of the Translator," 256.

12. Benjamin, "The Task of the Translator," 257.

13. De Man, "'Conclusions,'" 81–82.

14. Matthews, "What Did Archimedes Mean?" 149.
15. Warren, *The Art of Translation*, 7.
16. Barthes, *The Pleasure of the Text*, 61.
17. Simon, *Gender in Translation*, 15.
18. Donoghue, "Translation in Theory," 251.
19. Yeats, "The Symbolism of Poetry," 158.
20. Benjamin, "The Task of the Translator," 254.

Connoisseurs of Loneliness

1. Ruskin, *Modern Painters*, 112.

A Solving Emptiness

1. McClatchy, "The Art of Poetry XLI," 204−5.
2. Yeats, "The Symbolism of Poetry," 156−57.
3. McClatchy, "The Art of Poetry XLI," 204−5.

In a Glass, Darkly

1. Merrill, *The Changing Light at Sandover*, 199, 247.
2. Merrill, *The Changing Light at Sandover*, 239.

Works Cited

A Toy Balloon, the Man-Moth's Tear, and a Sack of Ripe Tomatoes

Bishop, Elizabeth. *The Complete Poems, 1927–1979*. New York: Farrar, Straus & Giroux; Noonday Press, 1991.

Keats, John. *The Letters of John Keats*. Ed. Hyder E. Rollins. Cambridge: Harvard University Press, 1958.

Moore, Marianne. *The Complete Poems of Marianne Moore*. New York: Penguin, 1986.

Salinger, J. D. *Franny and Zooey*. Boston: Little, Brown, 1961.

———. *Nine Stories*. Boston: Little, Brown, 1965.

———. *Seymour—An Introduction*. New York: Bantam, 1963.

On the Memory of Stone

Jeffers, Robinson. *The Selected Poetry of Robinson Jeffers*. New York: Random House, 1959.

A Story of Poetry and Poets

Barthes, Roland. *A Lover's Discourse*. New York: Hill and Wang, 1978.

Blanchot, Maurice. "The Gaze of Orpheus." In *The Gaze of Orpheus and Other Essays*. Trans. Lydia Davis. Barrytown: Station Hill, 1981.

Calasso, Roberto. *The Marriage of Cadmus and Harmony*. Trans. Kim Parks. New York: Knopf, 1993.

Cixous, Hélène. *Three Steps on the Ladder of Writing*. Trans. Sarah Cornell and Susan Sellers. New York: Columbia University Press, 1993.

H. D. (Hilda Doolittle). *Collected Poems, 1912–1944*. Ed. Louis Martz. New York: New Directions, 1983.

Ovid. *Metamorphoses*. Trans. Rolfe Humphries. Bloomington: Indiana University Press, 1955.

Rilke, Rainer Maria. "Orpheus. Eurydice. Hermes." In *The Selected Poetry of Rainer Maria Rilke.* Ed. and trans. Stephen Mitchell. New York: Vintage, 1984.

Sewell, Elizabeth. *The Orphic Voice.* New Haven: Yale University Press, 1960.

Virgil. *The Georgics.* Trans. L. P. Wilkinson. New York: Viking Penguin, 1982.

Writing the Poet, Unwriting the Poem

Eliot, T. S. "Little Gidding." In *The Complete Poems and Plays, 1909–1950.* New York: Harcourt, Brace & World, 1971.

Nabokov, Vladimir. *Lectures on Literature.* New York: Harcourt, Brace & Jovanovich, 1982.

Shelley in Ruins

Shelley, Percy Bysshe. *Shelley's Poetry and Prose: Authoritative Texts, Criticism.* Ed. Donald H. Reiman and Sharon B. Powers. New York: Norton, 1977.

Stevens, Wallace. *The Collected Poems of Wallace Stevens.* New York: Random House, Vintage, 1982.

Turner, A. Richard. *Inventing Leonardo.* New York: Knopf, 1992.

Wilde, Oscar. *The Artist as Critic.* Ed. Richard Gillman. New York: Random House, 1969.

Eating the Angel, Conceiving the Sun

Butts, William, ed. *Conversations with Richard Wilbur.* Jackson: University Press of Mississippi, 1990.

Eliot, T. S. *The Waste Land.* In *The Complete Poems and Plays, 1909–1950.* New York: Harcourt, Brace & World, 1971.

Heidegger, Martin. "The Thinker as Poet." In *Poetry, Language, Thought.* Trans. Albert Hofstadter. New York: Harper Row, 1975.

———. *What Is Called Thinking?* Trans. Jay Glenn Gray. New York: Harper Colophon, 1968.

Hendry, J. F. *The Sacred Threshold: A Life of Rainer Maria Rilke*. Manchester: Carcanet, 1983.

Rilke, Rainer Maria. "Archaic Torso of Apollo." In *The Selected Poetry of Rainer Maria Rilke*. Ed. and trans. Stephen Mitchell. New York: Vintage, 1984.

———. *Letters of Rainer Maria Rilke, 1910–1926*. Trans. Jane Barnard Greene and M. D. Herter Norton. New York: Norton, 1969.

———. *Duino Elegies*. Trans. J. B. Leishman and Stephen Spender. New York: Norton, 1963.

Stevens, Wallace. *The Collected Poems of Wallace Stevens*. New York: Random House, Vintage, 1982.

———. *Letters of Wallace Stevens*. New York: Knopf, 1963.

Valéry, Paul. *The Art of Poetry*. Vol. 7 of *The Collected Works of Paul Valéry*. Ed. Jackson Mathews. Trans. Denise Folliot. Bollingen 45. Princeton: Princeton University Press, 1958.

Divine Hunger

(Sources for the quotations are listed by section number and by order within each section.)

EPIGRAPHS:

Titus Lucretius Carus. *De rerum natura*. New York: G. P. Putnam's Sons, 1924. Bk. 1, line 36; bk. 4, lines 864–65, 1039, 1055.

George Herbert. "Love" (III). In *The Poems of George Herbert*. New York: Oxford University Press, 1961.

NUMBERED SECTIONS:

1. A. Meston. *Report on the Government Scientific Expedition to the Bellenden-Ker Range;* quoted in David R. Harris, "Aboriginal Subsistence in a Tropical Rain Forest Environment: Food Procurement, Cannibalism, and Population Regulation in Northeastern Australia," in *Food and Evolution: Toward a Theory of Human Food Habits*, ed. Marvin Harris and Eric B. Ross (Philadelphia: Temple University Press, 1987), 370.

2. Saint Augustine. *Confessiones*. Oxford: Clarendon, 1992. Bk. 2, ch. 6.

3. Genesis 3:6 (King James Version); François Rabelais. *Gargan-tua.* Paris: Minard, 1970. Bk. 1, ch. 5; Henry Fielding. *Tom Jones.* Bk. 6, ch. 1.

4. Diego Rodríguez de Silva y Velázquez. *The Rokeby Venus;* Robert Conquest. "The Rokeby Venus." Stanza 1, line 4.

5. Judges 14:14 (King James Version).

6. Lewis Carroll. *Alice's Adventures in Wonderland.* Ch. 7.

8. Luke 2:7 (King James Version).

11. Walt Whitman. "I Sing the Body Electric" ("Poem of the Body"). In *Complete Poetry and Selected Prose.* Ed. James E. Miller Jr. Boston: Houghton Mifflin, 1959.

12. 1 Peter 2:2 (King James Version).

13. Shakespeare. *Love's Labour's Lost.* Act 5, scene 1.

14. Simone Weil. "Spiritual Autobiography." In *Waiting for God.* Trans. Emma Craufurd. New York: Harper & Row, 1973. 69.

15. Shakespeare. *Othello.* Act 3, scene 4.

16. Hélène Cixous. "Coming to Writing." In *"Coming to Writing" and Other Essays.* Ed. Deborah Jenson. Trans. Sarah Cornell et al. Cambridge: Harvard University Press, 1991. 24.

17. Sir Francis Bacon. "Of Studies." In *The Essayes or Counsels, Civill and Morall.* Ed. Michael Kiernan. Cambridge: Harvard University Press, 1985. 153.

18. Friedrich Nietzsche. "Old and New Tables" (no. 16). In *Thus Spake Zarathustra.* Trans. Thomas Common. New York: Modern Library, 1978. 230.

22. Jan Kott. *The Eating of the Gods: An Interpretation of Greek Tragedy.* Trans. Boleslaw Taborski and Edward J. Czerwinski. New York: Random House, 1973. 197.

23. Mircea Eliade. *Myths, Rites, Symbols: A Mircea Eliade Reader.* Ed. Wendell C. Beane and William G. Doty. New York: Harper & Row, 1976.

24. Genesis 3:19 (King James Version).

26. Sigmund Freud. "Totem and Taboo." In *The Freud Reader.* Ed. Peter Gay. New York: Norton, 1989. 500–501.

27. Peter Farb and George Armelagos. *Consuming Passions: The Anthropology of Eating.* Boston: Houghton Mifflin, 1980. 119, 134–37, 165.
28. Shakespeare. *Othello.* Act 1, scene 3.
29. Anthèlme Brillat-Savarin. "Aphorismes pour servir de prolégomènes" (no. 4). In *Physiologie du Goût.* Paris: Garnier Frères, 1860.
32. Michel de Montaigne. "On the Cannibals." In *Four Essays.* Trans. M. A. Screech. New York: Penguin, 1995. 18–19.
33. Ezekiel 2:6.
34. Peggy Reeves Sanday. *Divine Hunger: Cannibalism as a Cultural System.* Cambridge: Cambridge University Press, 1986. 196, 210–11.
35. James Atlas. "The Literary Life." *The New Yorker.* 13 Oct. 1997. 38.
37. Titus Lucretius Carus. *The Nature of Things.* Trans. Anthony M. Esolen. Baltimore: Johns Hopkins University Press, 1995. Bk. 3, line 232.
38. Homer. *The Odyssey.* Trans. Robert Fagles. New York: Penguin, 1996. Bk. 11, lines 252–53.
39. Ralph Waldo Emerson. *Journals and Miscellaneous Notebooks.* Ed. William H. Gilman et al. Vol. 9. Cambridge: Harvard University Press, Belknap Press, 1960–82.

"Into the Unknown to Find the New"

Bachelard, Gaston. *The Poetics of Space.* Trans. Maria Jolas. New York: Orion Press, 1964.
Baudelaire, Charles. *Les Fleurs du Mal.* Trans. Richard Howard. Boston: David R. Godine, 1983.
Heidegger, Martin. "What are Poets For?" In *Poetry, Language, Thought.* Trans. Albert Hofstadter. New York: Harper & Row, 1975.
Hopkins, Gerard Manley. *The Poems of Gerard Manley Hopkins.* Ed. W. H. Gardner and N. H. MacKenzie. New York: Oxford University Press, 1967.
Kafka, Franz. "The Hunter Gracchus." In *Parables and Paradoxes.* Ed. Nahum N. Glatzer. Trans. Willa and Edwin Muir. New York: Schocken, 1975.

Sartre, Jean-Paul. *Baudelaire.* Trans. Martin Turnell. New York: New Directions, 1967.

Valéry, Paul. *The Art of Poetry.* Vol. 7 of *The Collected Works of Paul Valéry.* Ed. Jackson Mathews. Trans. Denise Folliot. Bollingen 45. Princeton: Princeton University Press, 1958.

À la Recherche de la Poésie Perdue

Barthes, Roland. *The Pleasure of the Text.* Trans. Richard Miller. New York: Farrar, Straus & Giroux, 1975.

Benjamin, Walter. "The Task of the Translator." In *Selected Writings: 1913–1926.* Ed. Marcus Bullock and Michael W. Jennings. Vol. 1. Cambridge: Harvard University Press, 1996.

Biguenet, John, and Rainer Schulte, eds. Introduction to *The Craft of Translation.* Chicago: University of Chicago Press, 1989.

Burnshaw, Stanley, ed. Introduction to *The Poem Itself.* New York: Holt, Rinehart and Winston, 1960.

De Man, Paul. "'Conclusions': Walter Benjamin's 'The Task of the Translator.'" In *The Resistance to Theory.* Theory and History of Literature, vol. 33. Minneapolis: University of Minnesota Press, 1986.

Donoghue, Denis. "Translation in Theory and in a Certain Practice." In *The Art of Translation.* Ed. Rosanna Warren. Boston: Northeastern University Press, 1989.

Frame, Donald. "Pleasures and Problems of Translation." In *The Craft of Translation.* Ed. John Biguenet and Rainer Schulte. Chicago: University of Chicago Press, 1989.

Johnson, Barbara. "Taking Fidelity Philosophically." In *Difference in Translation.* Ed. Joseph F. Graham. Cornell: Cornell University Press, 1985.

Matthews, Robert J. "What Did Archimedes Mean by '*khrysos*'?" In *Difference in Translation.* Ed. Joseph F. Graham. Cornell: Cornell University Press, 1985.

Simon, Sherry. *Gender in Translation.* New York: Routledge, 1996.

Tomlinson, Charles. "The Presence of Translation: A View of English Poetry." In *The Art of Translation.* Ed. Rosanna Warren. Boston: Northeastern University Press, 1989.

Warren, Rosanna, ed. Introduction to *The Art of Translation: Voices from the Field*. Boston: Northeastern University Press, 1989.

Wheatley, Phillis. *Poems of Phillis Wheatley*. Bedford MA: Applewood Books, 1995.

Wordsworth, William. "Preface to the Second Edition of the *Lyrical Ballads*." In *Selected Poems and Prefaces*. Ed. Jack Stillinger. Boston: Houghton Mifflin, 1965.

————. *The Prelude*. London: Penguin Books, 1971.

Yeats, William Butler. "The Symbolism of Poetry." In *Essays and Introductions*. New York: Macmillan, Collier Books, 1986.

Connoisseurs of Loneliness

Barthes, Roland. *The Pleasure of the Text*. Trans. Richard Miller. New York: Farrar, Straus & Giroux, 1975.

Bishop, Elizabeth. *The Complete Poems, 1927–1979*. New York: Farrar, Straus & Giroux; Noonday Press, 1991.

Lowell, Robert. *History*. New York: Farrar, Straus & Giroux, 1973.

Ruskin, John. *Modern Painters*. In *The Literary Essays of John Ruskin*. Ed. Harold Bloom. New York: DaCapo Press, 1965.

Schuyler, James. *Collected Poems*. New York: Farrar, Straus & Giroux, 1993.

A Solving Emptiness

McClatchy, J. D. "The Art of Poetry XLI." *Paris Review* 13.113 (winter 1989). [interview with Charles Wright]

Williams, C. K. *Flesh and Blood*. New York: Farrar, Straus & Giroux, 1987.

Wright, Charles. *Zone Journals*. New York: Farrar, Straus & Giroux, 1988.

Yeats, William Butler. "The Symbolism of Poetry." In *Essays and Introductions*. New York: Macmillan, Collier Books, 1986.

In a Glass, Darkly

Hall, Donald. "Poetry and Ambition." In *The Pushcart Prize, IX: Best of the Small Presses, 1984 – 85*. Wainscott NY: Pushcart Press, 1985.

Des Pres, Terrence. "Self / Landscape / Grid." In *The Pushcart Prize, IX: Best of the Small Presses, 1984−85.* Wainscott NY: Pushcart Press, 1985.

Merrill, James. *The Changing Light at Sandover.* New York: Atheneum, 1983.

Palgrave, Francis Turner. *The Golden Treasury: Second Series.* New York: Grosset & Dunlap, 1897.

About the Author

Sherod Santos is the author of four books of poetry: *Accidental Weather, The Southern Reaches, The City of Women,* and, most recently, *The Pilot Star Elegies,* which was a finalist for the National Book Award and the *New Yorker* Book Award. In 1999 he received an Academy Award for Literary Excellence from the American Academy of Arts and Letters. His other awards include the Delmore Schwartz Memorial Award, the B. F. Connors Prize from *The Paris Review,* an appointment as the Robert Frost Poet, and the Discovery/*The Nation* Award. He has received fellow-ships from the Guggenheim and Ingram Merrill foundations and the National Endowment for the Arts. He is currently Professor of English and Director of the Center for the Literary Arts at the University of Missouri–Columbia.

Index